The Christian Olympics

Going for the Gold Crowns

S.E. Gregg

Copyright © 2006, 2017 by S.E. Gregg
Published in 2017 Rev. ed. by Sound Doctrine Christian Ministries
Published in 2006 by Xulon Press
E-book ISBN: 978-0-9658587-2-4
Audible book ASIN: B01INZ5PTY

The Christian Olympics
by S.E. Gregg

Printed in the United States of America

Pbk ISBN:978-0-9658587-1-7

Library of Congress Control Number: 2016920626

All rights reserved solely by the author. The author guarantees all contents are original and do not infringe upon the legal rights of any other person or work. No part of this book may be reproduced in any form without the permission of the author.

All scripture quotations and references are from the King James Version of the Holy Bible unless otherwise stated. Publishers: American Bible Society and The World Publishing Company. Scripture marked NKJV: Scripture taken from the New King James Version. Copyright © 1979, 1980, 1982 by Thomas Nelson, Inc. Used by permission. All rights reserved.

www.SoundDoctrineMinistries.org

Praise for The Christian Olympics

"I endorse Gregg's book because it not only clearly outlines THE faith, but gives much needed knowledge of the rules of the race and why we as believers in Jesus Christ must fight on with life and press on with running the "race" - the 2000 year old Christian Olympics" **Caryl Matrisciana, Film Maker and Best Selling Author**

"An impressive spiritual guide with solid reasoning and sound logic, The Christian Olympics is highly recommended reading for anyone seeking to bolster the strength of their personal faith. Kudos to Gregg for producing such a standout inspirational volume that readers of all ages will surely appreciate." **Dominique Sessons, Apex Reviews**

"We are all participants in the Great Race. Some are maintaining their easy stride, some are limping along, some barely walking. I think I've been in all three in different times in my life. If you want to get to the finish line with those golden crowns waiting for you, you'll do yourself a big favor by reading this book. It'll challenge you for sure!" **Robert J. Shaw, Voice Over Artist, Narrator and Radio Show Host**

Praise for The Christian Olympics

"From the first trumpet call of the extravaganza to the Opening Ceremony, S. E. Gregg captures the contagious excitement and the competitive spirit of the Olympic games in the book "The Christian Olympics: Going for the Gold Crowns." The reader experiences vicariously the thrill of participation in the competition and training, and more importantly learns spiritual lessons for athletes in the Christian race. Gregg's writing is entertaining, inspirational, and motivating. The Christian Olympics" is expressive, Biblically sound, and challenging. Let the Games Began!" **Richard R. Blake, Christian Education Instructor, Book Store Owner and Writer**

"This is a book every person, everywhere must read to be inspired and equipped to run this race and not get weary!" **Marina Woods, Founder and Editor-in-Chief at Good Girl Book Club**

"S.E., your book is very well done." **PW-Pat Williams, Orlando Magic**

Dedication

To all marathon runners in the Christian Olympics:

And let us not be weary in well doing: for in due season we shall reap, if we faint not.
—Gal. 6:9

But they that wait upon the LORD shall renew their strength; they shall mount up with wings as eagles; they shall run, and not be weary; and they shall walk, and not faint.
—Isa. 40:31

Therefore, my beloved brethren,

be ye steadfast, unmovable, always abounding in the work of the Lord, forasmuch as ye know that your labor is not in vain in the Lord.
—1 Cor. 15:58

Let's "Go for the Gold Crowns!"

Table of Contents

Introduction 9

Chapter 1
   The Opening Ceremony 11

Chapter 2
   The Players in the Competitions 15

Chapter 3
   The Training and Discipline 27

Chapter 4
   Planning Strategies 37

Chapter 5
   The Competitions 65
   Part One: Getting Equipped 65
   Part Two: Let the Games Begin! 76

Chapter 6
   The Suffering 85
   Part One: Good or Bad? 85
   Part Two: The Workout 96

Chapter 7
The Closing and Rewards Ceremonies 131

Epilogue
The Competition That Made the Judge Stand Up......157

Pray This Prayer ……………………………………....159

Introduction

The idea for this book was gleaned from a newspaper article I wrote titled "The Christian Olympics Are Still Going On!" which was published in the Philadelphia *Sunday Sun*, on May 26, 2002.
The article explains that although the "Olympics begin and end, 'The Christian Olympics,' are still going on.... The Olympics is the most prominent international athletic competition in the world. Every fourth year (for the summer or winter games), athletes come from all over the world (to a selected city) to compete in a variety of sporting events. The opening ceremonies begin with a huge extravaganza. Athletes from all over the world march into a huge stadium waving the flags of their countries. The opening salutations include trumpets playing, Olympic flag with symbols raised, anthem sung, and an oath recited."

The article goes on to say, "The games begin, and the medal ceremonies take place after each final event. The top three finishers receive a gold, silver, or bronze medal while standing on a two-level platform. The competitions last for about sixteen days and conclude with the closing ceremony. All of the athletes march into the stadium together, the anthem is sung, and after hours of entertainment, the flames are extinguished," which concludes the Olympic Games.

For the very first time since the ancient Olympic Games were held in Greece, the 2004 Summer Games were held there where they all began, which was another inspiration for writing this book. In addition, there are many references in the New Testament to cities in ancient Greece. In fact, the apostle Paul preached and traveled as a missionary in many of the cities that would host the ancient games. Many churches were started in Greece. As the apostle Paul would view the ancient games, which dated back to the eighth century B.C., he saw that the athletic contest was very similar to the Christian race or competition. He made several references to the ancient games in the New Testament, comparing them to our service and walk with God—which is what we will do in this book, so that as Christians we can better understand our Christian race or competition.

CHAPTER 1

The Opening Ceremony

According to the *World Book 2000*, the most dramatic event in the opening ceremony of the Olympic Games is the moment that the Olympic flame is lit. The fire is always ignited in Olympia, Greece. In a torch relay, runners transport the flames from Greece to the site in the country that is hosting the games. Finally, the last runner reaches the stadium and lights the kettle. The flames burning remain until the closing ceremony, and then they are extinguished.

There are many preparations that take place before the Olympic Games begin. Contestants have been in training for at least four years and have to abide by strict regulations. The International Olympic Committee approves of the sports and events to be included in the games. They also determine the host cities, the Olympic competitions, and the eligibility of the athletes.

Webster's New World Dictionary defines the Olympic Games in ancient Greece as a festival with various contests held every four years at Olympia in honor of Zeus, which is the origin of the modern Olympic Games of international athletic competition. The modern competitions were held every four years at a selected city, the first at Athens in

1896. In the 1990s the summer and winter games were divided into cycles so they could be two years apart.

Just as the ancient Olympic Games had their first opening ceremony in Greece and was centered on religion, the Christian Olympics began about two thousand years ago in Jerusalem fifty days after the resurrection of Jesus Christ, on the day of Pentecost. The disciples and other followers of Christ were sitting together when suddenly the sound like a rushing mighty wind came from heaven "...and it filled all the house where they were sitting." (Acts 2:2). And they saw tongues that looked like flames of fire that rested on each of them. Then they were filled with the Holy Spirit, who enabled them to speak in other tongues (languages), one of the wonderful works of God (see Acts 1 and 2).

This was the "divine" opening ceremony. Just as the modern Olympic Games begin by lighting a flame of fire, the fire that symbolizes the Holy Spirit opened the Christian Olympics. Jesus Christ had ascended bodily back to heaven just ten days before the Holy Spirit came from heaven to baptize believers into the body of Christ and to dwell in the followers of Christ. Christianity and the Christian Olympics then began. On that day about three thousand people became Christians and entered the Christian race or Olympics. They confessed and believed in their hearts what they heard, that Jesus Christ, the Son of God, died for their sins, was buried, and rose bodily from the grave (1 Cor. 15:3–4, Rom. 10:9). Then they were initiated into the Christian race through water baptism, a public declaration that their old self or nature was crucified with Christ. When they came out of the water, it was a symbol that they had risen with Him and had a new life in Christ.

Now, about two thousand years later, people from every nation are becoming Christians and entering into the Christian Olympics daily. During the apostle Paul's missionary journeys in Greece he planted churches in cities

The Christian Olympics

such as the ones in Philippi, Thessalonica, and Corinth. (Acts 16:12; Acts 17 and 18). The Holy Spirit divinely inspired him to write epistles (letters) to these and other churches, which appear in the New Testament in the Bible, including the first epistle to the Corinthians, the second epistle to the Corinthians, the epistle to the Philippians, the first epistle to the Thessalonians, and the second epistle to the Thessalonians.

While he was in some of the cities, he would watch the ancient Greek contests and games that took place in their stadiums or arenas. While watching, The Holy Spirit revealed to him that this is what the Christian life is like. It is similar to the Greek contest; it is a Christian race or Christian Olympics. Paul began to preach and teach what was revealed to him. Throughout his letters to the churches, he would make mention of these contests and games by comparing them to the Christian life and walk.

Get Ready, Get Set, Go

The Christian race is a running and fighting competition. By having an understanding of these games we can glean more insight as to what the Christian life or race is all about. Whereas the athletes have to practice disciplining their whole being to enhance their athletic abilities to win the prize, Christians have to discipline their hearts, souls, minds, and strength towards faithful, loving, service toward God to win the prize.

CHAPTER 2

The Players in the Competitions

Contestants in the Olympic Games come from all over the world to compete with one another. They are called "spectacles" and competitors. They have passed all of the requirements and athletic training necessary to qualify to be contestants. Their main objectives are to be "faster, higher, stronger" than their competitors to win the gold medals.

Spectacles

In the Christian Olympics, we are also called spectacles, according to 1 Corinthians 4:9. The Greek word for spectacle means "one to be gazed at and made sport of." It can also mean a public show or theater. As Christians, we are on display to be gazed upon (Heb. 10:33) and looked over. We are a show. We should not be surprised that we are watched all the time, everywhere we go and in everything that we do. This should not bother us once we understand, as the apostle Paul did, that we are spectacles.

Were you thinking what I was thinking about the definition "to be gazed at and made sport of?" I was thinking about being teased and made fun of. Have you ever been ridiculed, bullied around, or picked on because you are a

Christian? It's only a reminder—so that we never forget—that we are still strangers and pilgrims in this world and spectacles in the Christian Olympics. The competitions are not over yet. We will always stand out like specs (smile), which is probably where the word spectacles came from.

Maybe this is how Paul felt in 1 Corinthians 4:9, according to the New International Version, which states that Paul felt that God had put the apostles on display at the end of a procession, like men condemned, dying in an arena. Paul is not complaining, but he wanted us to know how severely the apostles suffered as spectacles in this world. Did you notice in the definition that spectacles are not spectators?

As Christians in the Christian Olympics we cannot watch each other—watching where everyone goes and seeing what everyone is doing—and still be called spectacles. We have a tendency to make a portion of the Christian community spectacles, while we become the spectators sitting down watching. We follow them instead of putting on our own public show. We have to be careful of groups, events, and gatherings that lure us into making them spectacles while forcing us to become spectators. We must also watch that we do not ridicule one another and make fun of each other. Remember, we are not spectators, so we should not treat each other as such. No one in the Christian Olympics is a spectator, but we are all spectacles.

A final point: the spectacles in the Olympic Games are athletes that come from a diversity of backgrounds and from nations all over the world. They speak different languages and have various shades of skin color. It is the same of the spectacles in the Christian Olympics; they consist of an array of various skin tones, languages, cultures, and backgrounds from all over the world.

Spectators

When there are spectacles present we can be assured that

there will always be spectators. A spectator is someone who sees or watches an event without taking an active part in it—in other words an onlooker. The spectators in the Olympic Games are hundreds, thousands, and millions of onlookers watching the spectacles put on a public show of athletic abilities. In the Christian Olympics, there are several types of spectators. In 1 Corinthians 4:9, we find that spectators are the world, angels, and men in the Christian Olympics. From 1 Peter 1:12, we see that the angels, who are God's messengers, observe and watch the spectacles. They also minister to us (Heb. 1:13–14). They are the only spectators who are there to help in the race.

Remember when Satan went to God? It's recorded in Job, chapters 1 and 2. He came along with the sons of God when they went to present themselves to the Lord. The Lord asked Satan where he had come from, and he said that he had been going back and forth and walking up and down on the earth. When the Lord asked him if he considered His servant Job, Satan made it clear that he already knew about him. It was evident by Satan's answers that he had been watching Job for a very long time. He knew where he lived, his marital status, how many children he had, how many animals he had, and everything that he owned. Not only did he watch Job; he is also an onlooker watching every Christian, because he is another spectator in the Christian Olympics.

According to Revelation 12:10, Satan is a regular spectator, on the job twenty-four hours a day, seven days a week, to accuse or speak against the spectacles—to say things to God as he said about Job, that Job did not fear God for no reason. In other words, he is telling God that He had given him everything and had protected him, which was why Job served Him. Satan is now saying the same thing about us to God. "You have given them families, material things, and protection,and that's the only reason they serve You ....Oh, they don't love You, they just want what they can get from

You. Take all of that away, and You will see what I mean—they will curse You to Your face."

All of us could probably think of a few things that Satan tells God about our motives for serving Him: "They just taught that lesson to be patted on the back; they did not do it because they love You ....When they prayed in public, they just wanted to sound good; they didn't want You to hear them." Hopefully, every time Satan accuses us, we always prove him wrong, as Job did.

Competitors

In the Olympic Games the athletes compete with one another according to the sporting events and categories. For example, all of the runners will compete against other runners and the boxers against other boxers. They will try to be better so they can beat their competitors and win. There is a big difference, though, between the competitors of the Olympic Games and the Christian Olympics. Competitors usually compete against each other, but not in the Christian Olympics. The preachers do not compete against other preachers. The teachers do not compete against other teachers, nor do missionaries compete against other missionaries or one choir member against another—musicians against other musicians and so on and so on.

The church member we sat next to last Sunday is not our competitor. The ushers from other churches are not competitors with the ushers from our church. Neither are the soloists competing against each other.

Some Christians have the wrong idea about who our competitors are—the way that they look at one another and try to do something better, faster, or ahead of someone else. Or maybe they don't help one another in ministry because they are afraid that if they do, that ministry may grow larger than theirs.

That brings to mind another difference between the

competitors of the two different types of games. The Olympic Games are very self-serving for some athletes; it's every man or woman for himself or herself. If you are not on their team, they don't care what happens to you as long as you get out of their way so they can win the contest. If or when their competitor stumbles or falls, it only helps them get closer to winning the gold. That is part of the game, though; if contestants stopped to help others they would jeopardize their chance of winning. Besides, the judges would not allow it. With some athletes, if it was in their power to cause their competitors to fall or stumble—and get away with it—they would do it.

This is not the way that God wants Christians to compete in the Christian Olympics. Part of the contest involves helping one another. If we see a brother or sister stumbling or falling we are to help them get back up again (see Gal. 6:1–2). We could be the next one falling and may need assistance in getting back up. By the way, verse 2 tells us also to bear one another's burdens. You may ask, "Why would God want us to help our fellow competitors in the contest? That would only slow us down and keep us from winning the prize."

It's because our competition in not against one another. Once we realize this, it will put a new perspective on the Christian life. We don't have to put our foot out to make someone fall. We don't have to scheme and tell lies to destroy someone's character. When someone new comes to the church or joins a Christian organization, we don't have to ignore them or roll our eyes at them for fear that they may take our position the way people in the world do. I repeat: our competitors are not one another.

Who is our competition, then, if it is not the Christians we work with, fellowship with, and walk with every day? The competition in the Christian Olympics is not against one another but against Satan, the flesh, and the world (see Eph.

6:11–18, Gal. 5:16–26, and 1 John 2:15–17). We should be fighting against our threefold competition—the devil, the flesh, and the world—and not each other. How can we win the Christian race if we do not know who our competition is? One thing about the athletes in the Olympic Games: they know who they are competing against. They have to treat their fellow competitors as their worst enemies emotionally, physically, and psychologically. They study their scoring history, how they train, and everything about them. We, as Spectacles in the Christian Olympics, must do the same.

Satan

We mentioned earlier about Satan being our spectator or onlooker and accusing us 24/7. He is also our competitor. Did you think of the same word I was thinking of? When I thought of competitor, the word predator came to my mind. It's a person or animal that robs, steals, and destroys. Wasn't Satan the one who robbed Adam and Eve of a blissful life, a life without worry and sin? Didn't he come in the form of a serpent crawling around on the earth tempting Eve to disobey God in Genesis? The answer to both questions is yes.

Let's get back to the word "competitor." Other words for competitor are opponent, antagonist, or rival. In the Olympic Games the spectators are not the competitors, but in the Christian Olympics some of them are both. Satan is our spectator and our competitor. Not only is he right beside us competing against us, he is also watching our every move from afar. We mentioned before how he watched Job so he knew how to attack Job, with God's permission, of course. Satan has the advantage of watching us and knowing what to tempt us with, while seeing where we are in the race. That is the advantage of being a competitor and a spectator at the same time.

It is a disadvantage, though, for the spectacles in the Christian Olympics to have spectators who are also competitors, which makes our competition far greater than the Olympic Games. In spite of this, God has given us the ability to win the race, which we will deal with later. Just think how it would be if those who were running in the Olympic Games could see how the other runners were running, as a spectator/competitor—how much of an advantage it would give them. They would know who to run in front of. Who is losing their breath? Who is slowing down? Who is catching up with them on the outside tracks and about to pass them? They could run a little faster to beat them and win the prize.

The Flesh

Our second competitor is the flesh. The Bible describes our old nature (our self) or our old man as the flesh. Before we became Christians our nature was ungodly, sinful, unrighteous, and condemned to death (see Rom. 3:23, 5:14, and 8:8). When we received the sacrificial death of Jesus Christ on the cross and His shed blood as payment in full for our sins, our sin debt of death was paid, and we were given the gift of eternal life (see Rom. 6:23). We now have a new life in Christ or a new nature. The old nature was crucified with Christ, because He took our place on the cross and in exchange gave us His life (see Rom. 6:6, Gal. 2:20). You may ask how the flesh, our old nature, could be our competitor when it was crucified with Christ. That's a very good question; let's see what God is telling us.

Once we became Christians we became spiritual beings—spiritually, we were crucified with Christ. As spiritual beings there are things that happened to us that we didn't see or feel, but we know that it happened because God said so. For example, when Jesus was explaining to Nicodemus in John 3 what being "born again" meant, He called the Spirit the wind. In verse 8 Jesus says that we hear the wind when it blows, but we cannot tell where it came from or where it went. This is how it is, says Jesus, for everyone who is born of the Spirit.

We have never seen God, but we believe in Him by faith. We know He is there by seeing His magnificent creation around us (see Rom. 1:20). In other words, what Jesus was saying to Nicodemus and to us is that His spiritual activities in our lives are not seen, but we are affected by them through faith. Everyone is born of the Spirit this way. Spiritually we have a new or spiritual nature. Our old nature was crucified, but we still live in our same bodies. It's our old bodies, our old flesh that still wants to keep doing the old sinful habits that they did before we were saved. We now have two natures: the old and the new nature, which are in a constant battle with each other.

Many believers have been living in their old flesh long enough to have gotten used to giving it whatever it demands—doing, acting, speaking, and living by those demands. Then when we are born again of the Holy Spirit, He tells us how to talk, act, speak, and live. This is where the battle comes in. Who are we going to obey—our old nature or the Holy Spirit? So the old nature or our flesh is our competitor.

The World

Our third competitor is the world, and is also our spectator. We mentioned before how Paul felt about the apostles being made a spectacle to the world. This is the same world that we compete against in the Christian Olympics. Everything in the world—our jobs, the government, and our communities—competes against us. According to 1 John 2:15–17, the lust of the flesh, the lust of the eyes, and the pride of life are things of the world. We are told not to love these things because if we do, the love of the Father will not be in us. The world will try to get us to love the world and not God. We can't have the love of the Father and the love of the world in us at the same time. We have to make a choice: who are we going to love? There are three areas in which the world competes with the spectacles. The first one we will discuss is the lust of the flesh.

lust of the flesh

The meaning for the Greek word for "lust" according to this verse is an "over desire." The world will try to get us to desire things too much in order to please our old fleshly nature. It will offer us all types of things to please our flesh. We are constantly bombarded by the world to buy something to feel good. "Wear this and you'll feel better....Drink this, and you will think better." If we follow the world to feed our flesh, we will develop an "over desire" to feed the flesh or give it what it demands. This is how the world catches us, and before you know it, we could be addicted to something. This is how people become addicted to drugs, alcohol, tobacco, sex, gambling, and other things.

lust of the eyes

Another way the world lures us away from God is through the things that the world shows us, the visual images the world proudly flashes before our eyes—things like violence, pornography, homosexuality, and other things. This brings to mind a commercial I saw not too long ago advertising either a mint or gum. In the commercial, a dog jumps on top of a man who had the product in his mouth and kisses him on the lips. The subliminal message was to show that sexual relationships between mankind and beast are acceptable. Why would a company that makes a product to make your breath fresh want to display this kind of a message? What do they have to do with each other? Nothing, but because God says in the books of Exodus, Leviticus, and Deuteronomy that "thou shall not lie with a beast," they want to go against God and try to show that there's nothing wrong with it.

We have to be so careful of what we look at and what is put before our eyes to view. The world's messages are subliminal; the world can keep showing us things, and eventually we become hooked and begin to tolerate it. For example, they have shown on television two women kissing each other on the lips so much that now it is accepted. The subliminal message is that homosexuality is okay, when God says that it is against nature (see Rom. 1:26–27). Have you noticed that many television sitcoms have an episode about homosexuality or an actor playing a regular part as a homosexual?

pride of life

Another of the world's lures has to do with the pride of life. The Greek word for pride means vain boasting, glory, or ostentation. Ostentation in the English language means an outright display, showiness, and boastful exhibition. This brings to mind the time when Satan went to Jesus and told Him that if He would fall down and worship him he would give Him the kingdom (Matthew 4:1–11). The nerve of the devil to offer Jesus what He already owned! He created it! This only shows that Satan will try anything. The world is constantly offering us pieces of the pie but with an attachment to it—that is, to leave God out of the picture. They tell us that we don't need God. "We'll give you a mansion with seven garages for your six new luxury cars and a jet, oh, and an SUV, if you would only forget about all of that Jesus stuff."

That offer appeals to our pride. We imagine how we would look in our new mansion. We envision the expressions on our friends' faces when they see us with a new car for every day of the week. We can't even imagine how it would be to have a private jet available at our beck and call. If we let our pride get in the way of our love for the Father, we will deny Him and take the world's offer.

Sometimes pride is involved in a decision we make in our homes or on our jobs, situations when we are asked to look the other way. We pretend we are not Christians just to get more money for material gain. We know a product is made by a company that opposes Christian values, but we purchase it anyway because it saves us money. Again, all of this feeds into our pride to get more and to keep up with the Joneses.

The players in the Christian Olympics are the spectacles and their competitors are Satan, the flesh, and the world, with an array of spectators watching the competitions. As spectacles, our main objective is to finish our race to receive the gold crowns, and the task of our competitors is to prevent us from finishing and winning the prize.

CHAPTER 3

The Training and Discipline

We Train with Spiritual Exercises

Walking in the Spirit

Whereas the athletic training of the body is physical exercise, Christians train their bodies through spiritual exercises. Our first spiritual exercise is walking in the Spirit, found in Galatians 5:16–26. Since we have a new nature, we don't have to walk the same way that we walked in the old nature anymore. Since the Holy Spirit indwells us, we can now take each step under His control. With every step that we take, we have to ask ourselves: is this what the Holy Spirit wants me to say? Is this where He wants me to go? Is this what He wants me to do?

But we have to know what the Holy Spirit wants us to do, which leads us to the next two spiritual exercises, which are Bible study and prayer. We will not know how to walk without instructions. The Holy Bible gives us all the instructions we need to walk in the Spirit. But we have to study our instruction book to find our walking directions. Once we have them, then we pray for guidance and to be filled with the Holy Spirit (Ephesians.5:18) who enables us to follow those directions.

Walking by Faith

Then it is time to exercise our faith by putting into action what we have learned and prayed about. This is the spiritual exercise we must do consistently and regularly if we want to remain qualified to compete in the Christian Olympics. To get some idea of what it is like to walk by faith, the Holy Spirit gave us a list of our brothers and sisters who walked by faith, in the Book of Hebrews. The entire eleventh chapter is dedicated to those saints who demonstrated their faith. When they were given their walking directions and instructions they obeyed, even though sometimes it did not make sense, it sounded strange, and people made fun of them. Some were beaten, had no food, clothes, or shelter, or were even killed. But because of their faith in what God had promised them, though they could not see it, they still had hope it would come to pass, because "…faith is the substance of things hoped for, the evidence of things not seen." (Heb. 11:1)—faith that is exercised.

Let's look at the people who exercised faith in action: Abel offered God a more excellent sacrifice than his brother, Cain. Enoch pleased God and was translated that he should not see death (which meant that Enoch did not have to die to go to heaven, God transported him to heaven without using the vehicle of death. He was walking with God one day and he kept walking and walking until God took Him to heaven to be with Him. Genesis 5:22-24). When God warned Noah about the flood, even though he never saw rain, he began preparing an ark. Abraham left his father's home to live in a strange country, as God requested of him, even though he did not know where he was going. Sarah, his wife, received strength to conceive and bear a child in her old age, becoming the mother of multitudes. They all had faith in God's Promised Land, even though some never saw it come to pass.

Abraham passed his test when he offered up his son Isaac. God's request sounded strange to him, but he believed that God would raise him from the dead, knowing that God promised Isaac to him. Isaac, concerning things to come, blessed Jacob and Esau. Jacob, who was dying, blessed both of the sons of Joseph. These are examples of walking by faith. Walking by faith is walking by believing what God had promised would come true, even though it cannot be seen. "(For we walk by faith, not by sight:)" (2 Cor. 5:7).

Stretching by Faith

Have you ever taken a l-o- n-g s-t-r-e-t-c-h, maybe in the morning when you got up, and while yawning you extended your limbs to full length? Miraculously, the stretching seemed to wake you up. Or when your body was tired of being in one position and you stretched your limbs to full length, it seemed to put vitality in those limbs. Even though you went back to doing the same thing again, you felt revitalized. It helped you to go the distance until you reached that particular goal.

The athletes do this during training when their muscles get tired or to loosen them just before they perform. It's the same way with s-t-r-e-t-c-h-i-n-g by faith; after walking by faith, sometimes we have to walk a longer distance, but we are tired and we can't see the end ahead of us, so we stretch to get more strength to keep going. That is exactly what stretching by faith is: continuing to believe God's promises until they are fulfilled, even if we get tired of waiting. If we stop having faith in what God promised, we will never be able to stretch our faith, and we will become too weak to continue in the race. Look at Joseph: when he died, God's promise had not been fulfilled, yet he reminded the children of Israel again of the promise that God would bring them out of Egypt to the Promised Land.

Even though his father and his father's father and his father's father's father said the same thing and it still had not happened, he believed the promise. Even though he was on his deathbed and would never see it, he passed it on to his children's children's children—three generations. Then he told them what to do with his bones, stretching his faith again at death, and he died in faith. Let's call this "hand-me-down faith."

After his birth Moses was hidden for three months by his parents, who were not afraid of the king's commandments. Moses chose to suffer with his own people rather than to have privileges and treasures of being the son of Pharaoh's daughter. He had faith that God had better treasures to offer him than what Pharaoh could give him. Believing that God rewards those who diligently seek Him, he did not fear the wrath of the king when he left Egypt. He kept the firstborn of his people from being destroyed through the sprinkling of the blood and keeping the Passover. His people passed through the Red Sea on dry land. Here you can see how Moses' faith stretched all the way from choosing to suffer with his own people to crossing the Red Sea on dry land.

The walls of Jericho fell down after Joshua and the children of Israel walked around the city for seven days. Rahab, who was a harlot, did not perish with the other unbelievers in Jericho, because she helped Joshua's spies. They walked by faith and kept walking and walking and stretching their faith. And what more shall I say? Time would fail me to tell of:

"Gideon, and of Barak, and of Samson, and of Jephthah; of David also, and Samuel, and of the prophets: who through faith subdued kingdoms, wrought righteousness, obtained promises, stopped the mouth of lions, quenched the violence of fire, escaped the edge of the sword, out of weakness were made strong, waxed valiant in fight, turned to flight the armies of the aliens. Women received their dead raised to life again: and others were tortured, not accepting deliverance; that they might obtain a better resurrection: And others had trial of cruel mockings and scourgings, yea, moreover of bonds and imprisonment: They were stoned, they were sawn asunder, were tempted, were slain with the sword: they wandered about in sheepskins and goatskins; being destitute, afflicted, tormented; (of whom the world was not worthy:) they wandered in deserts, and in mountains, and in dens and caves of the earth." Hebrews 11:32–38.

God has made it much easier for us to live by faith, because He left records throughout the Bible, much more than what was just mentioned, of real people who walked and stretched their faith. It was much harder for them; they really stepped out into the unknown. They did not have groups of people to follow as examples, but because of them we now have examples to follow. This was why Hebrews 11 was written, so that we could see that we are surrounded with a great quantity of witnesses who give evidence and testimony to walking and stretching faith. So we must do our spiritual exercises daily by walking in the Spirit, walking and stretching our faith to run in the race.

Spiritual Discipline

Christians have to train, practice discipline, and obey the rules just as athletes do, or they will be disqualified. Listen to what the apostle Paul said about himself: "But I discipline my body and bring it into subjection, lest, when I have preached to others, I myself should become disqualified." (for the prize) 1 Cor. 9:27, NKJV. Paul admits that he has to practice discipline if he wants to win the prize. He realizes that even though he was preaching to others, he could lose his reward if he did not discipline his own body—a warning to those who serve others, whether in the ministry, in leadership, on the mission field, in the church, in the community, or in the home. Serving others is a task that requires looking at others and their needs and meeting those needs. By looking at others it is very difficult to see ourselves. If we are not careful we will stop training and practicing discipline. Leaders have a tendency to feel that they are all right. This is why many leaders fall into sin.

The discipline and training for the Christian Olympics includes prayer, Bible study, and fellowship with other Christians. Paul says that without discipline we will lose our prize. Why is discipline so important? Because without discipline we won't do our spiritual exercises, which will cause us to fall into sin and not finish the race.

Athletes physically train their bodies to do whatever they command them to do. When they want their legs, hands, feet, or other parts of their bodies to perform a particular task, they train it through exercise and discipline until they accomplish the desired goal. They go to great lengths in their discipline and training. They get up very early in the morning and exercise for hours. They are placed on a strict diet. They eliminate any activity that interferes with their grueling routines, even sexual activity.

We mentioned earlier how the apostle Paul said that he had to keep under his body, which means in the Greek to keep down or press under and bring it into subjection, which in turn means to lead into servitude—again, just like the athletes we have to discipline our feet, hands, tongue, mind, and whatever else to obey God. The old nature that we mentioned earlier wants to go in one direction, and our new nature wants to go God's way. We have to discipline ourselves to do the spiritual exercises to make our body do or go in the direction of our new nature.

When you read Paul's statement, can you visualize him hitting himself with a Bible verse to make his body do what his new nature was telling him to do? Paul is saying that our bodies do what we tell them to do by keeping the old nature down and in subjection to our new nature. This takes much practice and discipline, just like athletic training, because we have to discipline ourselves to do these spiritual exercises.

Lay Aside Every Weight and Sin

Athletes do not let anyone distract them from their race to the finish line. They ignore anything that will wear them down. Christians are admonished to "...lay aside every weight, and the sin which so easily ensnares us, ..." (Heb. 12:1, NKJV)—the sin that is standing around us.

Hebrews 12 starts off by reminding Christians of the "great cloud of witnesses" mentioned in chapter 11, which we discussed earlier—the testimony of those who walked and stretched their faith. Since we have this evidence of their testimonies as an example, we are admonished to put away every encumbering weight (which is what "lay aside every weight" means in the Greek) and sin. This means that there are many worldly and sensual things that can hinder our spiritual race.

There are many things that are pleasing to the eye, ear, and touch that we are easily influenced and affected by. If we begin to live to please our senses only, we will develop an appetite for those things and become addicted to them. For example, people who feed their visual senses by watching pornography eventually will have to continue to satisfy and please their visual senses with pornography. Then there are other addictions, whether they are drugs, alcohol, gambling, or other things, that become weights, because we can become hooked on them. They become a burden and a sin. They can literally keep our heads bowed because of the shame, by keeping us from looking up to God. It is also very difficult to run with our heads down. That is the reason why God never intended for us to live only to please our senses, because it will become more than just pleasing our senses. Instead, our senses will control us.

This reminds me of Eve when she was in the garden, recorded in Genesis. The devil appealed to her senses by telling her what would happen if she ate of the fruit that God had told her not to eat. God wants to save us from destroying ourselves, by living to please Him and not to please ourselves (2 Cor. 5:14-15). If we begin to enjoy pleasing our senses, that pleasure will become an addiction, a weight, a sin, and a burden, and it will hinder us from finishing our race. So we must lay down our burden of weights and sins.

Or maybe it's the music we listen to that pleases our senses, with the words or beat that echo in our ears things that are contrary to the Bible. But the music sounds good, and it makes us feel good. Soon it will dominate our thinking to the point that we will think like the world thinks and want to do the things that we are hearing, because how we think affects how we act. There is a lot of Christian music, yes, Christian music, that is very sensual. What I mean is that some of the music and the way it is sung tempts some people to move certain parts of their bodies in a sensual way, which arouses illicit sexual desires and can cause some people to sin.

The sins that are standing or lingering around us could be things in our homes that can cause us to sin. Maybe it's a particular television program that we have to stop looking at, or maybe we can't watch television at all if it causes us to sin. "Lay aside" also means to "put away" in the Greek. This may mean that we may have to throw away some of our books, magazines, music, and other things if they become a weight and cause us to sin. Maybe we will have to change the radio stations that we listen to.

Sometimes there are people who are hindering us. We may have to get new friends or be friendless for a while. Whatever the hindrance may be, we must lay it aside and put it away so we will have nothing to hinder our run in the race. This will take a tremendous amount of discipline, just like the disciplined life of an athlete.

Sins That Can Be Avoided

There are some sins that we can avoid just by not trying them. For example, if we have never been immoral, tried smoking, drinking, using drugs, gambling, pornography, and some other things, we will not have to worry about becoming addicted to them. Addictions become strongholds in our lives; they become what we live for every day and depend on instead of God. That is what makes them a sin. Plus, addictions usually lead to more sins against ourselves and others. It just makes it harder to lay aside sins of addictions to have a victorious run in the Christian race, so we are better off never trying anything that could become habit-forming.

CHAPTER 4

Planning Strategies

Running Well

There are principles in the Bible that we can follow that will help us to avoid many of these weights and sins before they begin. We will start with the family and develop strategies so that we can run our races well, just like athletes that put together and develop a game plan.

The family is the most significant group in the Christian Olympics because it is our foundation. Our families affect our communities and our churches, which is why the family is so important. Because the family is so important, this is where our competitors—the flesh, the world, and the devil—try to attack us. When our competitors succeed in destroying the family, it has a domino effect causing destruction to the community and the church, it affects our Christian race.

The most successful schemes that our competitors have developed (which they have been doing for centuries) to attack our families involve sexual temptations—the same old temptations that still entrap us as spectacles causing us to lose our boxing and wrestling matches in these areas. It seems as though we should have been able to overcome yielding to sexual temptations as a Christian community by now. Instead, it has gotten worse in the church, just like the world. Some of you may be thinking that sex is not the only problem. But because of yielding to this one particular temptation alone, it has made its way to being one of the leading causes of the breakup of families, divorce, unwanted pregnancies, delinquency, sexually transmitted diseases, violence, substance abuse, and other things, even among Christians.

When we are tempted to commit sexual sins, or any other sins, that is just what it is—a temptation. It is not a sin until we yield to that temptation (James 1:13–15). With those types of sins, we have a choice of whether or not we want to sin.

We may not be able to avoid being tempted, but all of us have a choice given to us by God, the power to choose whether or not we will yield to those temptations. There are strategies we can develop from the Scriptures that will make it easier to resist yielding to these temptations, thus winning our boxing and wrestling matches in these areas. The strategies we develop from the Scriptures will cause us to gain the victory over our competitors' schemes, just as the athletes put together a strategic game plan to beat their competition.

Sexual sins are defined in the Bible as having sexual relations with someone other than your husband or your wife, which means God approves of sexual relations only within the confines of marriage between a man and a woman. Any type of sexual relation outside the confines of marriage, a husband (a man) and his wife (a woman), is defined as fornication, according to 1 Corinthians 6:18. The Greek meaning for the word "fornication" in this verse has a general meaning, including all sexual sin.

This verse offers a strategic plan to use when tempted to

commit fornication, and that is to flee. Fleeing must be the first strategy to keep in our minds at all times, because our competitors will surprise us with the unexpected, and we won't have time to think with reason. By the time we try to rationalize what is happening in our minds, what we should say or do, it will be too late to avoid yielding to the temptation because it will happen so fast. We won't have time to think to ourselves, "I can't believe she just kissed me on my lips" or "Why is he putting his arms around my waist?" or "I didn't know she had feelings for me." (The way things are today, the temptation could come from someone of the same sex as we are.) We have to literally take off and run as fast as we can, just as Joseph did in Genesis 39:12.

Why is it so important to flee fornication? Because according to 1 Corinthians 6:18, if we commit fornication, it is the only sin in the Bible that we can commit against our own bodies, which are the temples of the Holy Spirit. That becomes a hindrance to running on the racetrack, because it will weigh us down like weights on our feet making it extremely difficult to run.

Then there is the strategy that has to be developed for the times when we have time to think and rationalize about sexual temptations, when we know we are being tempted sexually. For example, when someone openly invites us to commit a sexual sin and says, "Let's meet alone tonight after Bible study" or "Let's meet in your hotel room later, after the conference" or "Come over tonight after the children go to sleep." This is why we have to keep on our attire—the whole armor of God (The whole armor of God is explained in Ephesians 6:12-18. This passage gives a list of spiritual weapons to use in order to fight against the cunning methods of the devil.)— at all times so that we will have the power to stand against the deceptions of Satan. What we think at a time like that is crucial, and this is where the helmet of salvation can influence and guard our thoughts.

We must put in our mind the fact that if we commit this sexual sin, we will be sinning against our own body. Our bodies are the temple of the Holy Spirit, who is living inside us. Our bodies do not belong to us; we are not to do what we want to do with them. They belong to God, who bought us from Satan with the blood of Jesus Christ. Our bodies are intended to be used for the glory of God. I am a member of the body of Christ, and if I commit a sexual sin, I am taking the body of Christ along with me as I sin. Also, if I join my body to someone in a sexual sin, I become one flesh with them. Since I am a member of the body of Christ, I am joining the members of Christ in the sexual act itself (1 Cor. 6:13–20). Since my body is a member of Christ, if I commit fornication, the Holy Spirit is with me during the act. Arming ourselves with these strategic thoughts will unclog our thinking and help us not to yield to sexual temptations.

These strategic plans can be implemented in every walk of life, whether we are single, single parents, married, widowed, separated, or divorced. We will now implement them specifically to each group. First we will start with developing these strategies for married people in the area of sexual temptations.

Strategies for the Married

The Bible principle and strategy for married people to be obedient to God is not to have sexual relations outside of their marital bond. In fact, marriage is the only place for sexual relations to occur. A husband and wife are free to express their love to each other sexually on a regular basis, fulfilling each other's needs. They never have to go outside of the marital bond to be sexually fulfilled, because they are in the bond of marriage. When they are tempted to go outside this bond, they have the opportunity to make the choice whether or not to commit adultery. Well, you may be saying, it's not that simple. That is partly true, but yielding to this particular temptation starts long before the act is actually committed and that can be avoided.

For example, if a married person spends more time with a person of the opposite sex than with their spouse, develops intimacy with that person, and then commits adultery, this could have been avoided by not yielding to the temptation created by spending so much time together and by avoiding the development of intimacy between each other. Look at married movie stars; they are separated for months and sometimes years, filming or promoting movies. Some become so intimate with their co-stars that they commit adultery. Some go as far as falling in love and divorcing their spouses and marrying the co-star. Therefore a strategy for the married is **to avoid developing intimacy with those of the opposite sex.**

There are people in vocations that force husbands and wives to be away from each other for long periods of time. There are professional athletes, the military, political officeholders, musicians, recording artists, and others like executives who have to go out of town every weekend—even people in spiritual vocations like missionaries, evangelists, Bible teachers, preachers, gospel artists, entertainers, and others.

The Bible teaches that once two people are married, they have the duty to fulfill each other's needs sexually and on a regular basis (1 Cor. 7:3–5). In fact, according to verse 5, they are never to deprive one another of sex "except it be with consent for a time." The words "with consent" means *from united voice (Greek meaning)*. This means both married partners have to agree to deprive each other of sex and have a *fixed time* (Greek meaning) when they will resume regular sexual relations. If one spouse does not give consent, then there can be no agreement. The Scriptures even stipulate for what purpose a married couple can make this type of an agreement—only for fasting and prayer, and to come together again or *about the same time,* according to the Greek language, so that they won't be tempted by Satan for their "... incontinency" (verse 5). The biblical meaning for "incontinency" means to be absent of the virtue in restraining the sexual appetite, which means married couples do not have self-restraint with regard to sexual activity. And if they deprive one another, other than for the reasons that God has specified and for a fixed time, Satan can tempt them to commit adultery.

I can imagine what you maybe thinking: "What happens if a spouse becomes ill or is pregnant and cannot have sex? Isn't this depriving one another?" No, it's not the same thing; these are among the situations that are not the norm and are beyond their control. Therefore, God will give them grace in the area of sexual desire until the crisis is over. The big problem in marriages today, even among Christians, is that couples are not following the Scriptures in this area. This is why there are so many married couples committing adultery and so many divorces among Christians, all of which could have been avoided if couples refrained from depriving one another. One cannot expect to practice celibacy after getting married.

Marriages in our culture are more like two people who have the same name but live separate lives. The majority of married couples, whether Christians or non-Christians, are living single. For example, sometimes you cannot tell whether a woman is married or single because she ends up having to do everything by herself, whereas a married woman should not have all the responsibility on her. Some men are married, but you would never know it because you never see them with their wives; they simply leave them at home.

Another point I'd like to add about adultery: women especially get angry at the women their husbands committed adultery with. You have seen situations where the wife is in a rage of anger and wants to fight the other woman. A wise person once said: "That rage of anger should have been towards her husband—not saying that she should not have been angry with the other woman, but her husband knew that he was married and took a vow before God to be faithful to his wife. He was the one that broke his marriage vow, not the other woman."

Some wives even go as far as getting angry with women to whom their husbands may be attracted. It's not the women's fault that the husbands are attracted to them. Even with the kind of women that flirt with other women's husbands (which God-fearing women would never do), it is the husband's responsibility to ignore the advances and flirtations of other women. Sometimes the men may have to do more than just ignore them. For example, if a woman wants to fix his tie, he may have to say, "No, thank you, my wife can do that for me." After he does that a few times the woman will get the message, and he will be known as a man who is faithful to his own wife. Husbands, not their wives, have the responsibility to uphold their own integrity.

So we see that deprivation of sex is not for the married. The married couples in the Corinthian church were having this problem, which is why the apostle Paul addressed these issues in 1 Corinthians 7. Did you notice that 1 Corinthians 7:5 does not say that a couple can deprive each other of sex for God's work? "What, the preacher can't leave his wife for a week to preach a revival?" "The evangelist can't leave his family for six months while he wins souls for Christ?" "This can't be what God means!" But this is exactly what God means.

According to 1 Corinthians 7:33–34, the foremost responsibility of husbands and wives is their marriages and caring for each other and not the things of the Lord. The home and marriage come before service to the Lord outside of the home. "Wait just a minute now," you may be saying, "married people can serve God outside of the home." They can if their own homes are in order. Look at what Paul tells Timothy about the qualifications of the bishops and deacons in 1 Timothy 3:4–5. They must be able to rule their own houses well, because if they cannot, how can they take care of the church of God? Therefore, God will permit them to serve Him outside of the home only if their homes are in order and they don't deprive one another sexually.

So what God is telling us is that the pastor should take his wife along on that week-long revival. The evangelist should take his wife along with him for the six months he will be away winning souls for Christ. If that job takes a husband or wife out of town frequently, then the spouse must go also—and in some cases their children as well. I can hear what some of you are saying: "We work and have our careers together" or "We are in ministry together." But if both of you are actually married to your careers or your ministry and don't spend time on your relationship, you could still be defrauding one another.

Many rich people do not raise their own children, and some, like some of the children of missionaries, are shuttled off to boarding schools. Sometimes grandparents or other family members are given the responsibility to raise them. Many times these children feel abandoned and unloved, like orphans being raised by someone other than their own parents. Some grow up with many psychological problems and become vulnerable to the world's vices. This causes some Christian children to walk away from the Christian faith. Therefore vocations that keep parents away from their children or that keep married couples separated are really not designed for married couples.

The lifestyle of our families in today's culture promotes the separation of married couples and their children. This is what is leading to adultery, divorce, broken homes, and other things. Not only does it cause marriages to crumble, it also causes disobedient children and teenage delinquency.

Most of the time the situation is that fathers are never home to rule their own children because they are so busy outside the home serving God or busy pursuing their own careers and leaving their wives to handle the children alone.

They don't realize that the families God gave them are the careers and the ministries that they have chosen. If they wanted careers or ministries other than their families, then it would have been better if they had not gotten married. Whatever it takes for husbands to be home after work to be with their families, even if they have to give up their own careers, is what God is calling husbands to do today—as long as they can provide for the needs of their families so they will not be absent from the home.

Of course there are exceptions and circumstances in which this cannot be followed. But instead of this being an exception to the rule, today it is common practice for the fathers to be absent from the home, even in the Christian community. Then there are cases where both the husband and wife are fulfilling their own careers or are involved in ministry, with little time spent on their marriage or children. One spouse may say to the other, "If you can have your career [or ministry], so can I." Then they begin to compete and forget about their marriage and children. They have not made their homes their primary careers or ministry.

I am sure you have heard of politicians who have been politicking all of their lives or executives who have climbed corporate ladders who eventually begin to notice that they don't really know their own families. Then they make an announcement that they will resign or retire so they can spend more time with their families. Their children are grown and on their way to college, and never got to know their own fathers and sometimes their mothers. You have heard the speeches given by award recipients after receiving awards for their achievements. They thank their families for their support during the time they were working hard to win.

Most of the time, what they are really saying is that they had to sacrifice and neglect their family relationships in order to get that award. They are thanking their families for putting up with them and not abandoning them during the process.

This is so profound that if married Christians would follow the **strategic plan of not defrauding one another**, it could help avoid the very act of adultery and lower the divorce rate and stop the decline of the family structure, while they lay down the weight of this sin to have a victorious run in the Christian race.

Strategies for Parent(s)

Most of the athletes in the Olympic Games have been training in their particular sport since they were children. When everyone was outside playing, their parents had them at the gym practicing whatever skill they saw their children excel in. While other children were at the movies, they were at home exercising, doing things like push-ups and sit-ups. Their childhood was sacrificed because their parents had a goal. They were looking ahead and preparing their children for the Olympic Games so they could win the gold. How much more should Christian parents prepare their children for the Christian Olympics?

Would we dream of sacrificing our children's childhood for the Christian Olympics? If there is a movie that all the children in the neighborhood are going to see and it promotes violence and disrespect of authority, would we allow them to go, just because it is what the other children are doing? The movie could teach our children to be violent and to disrespect God and authority.

Do we encourage them to seek worldly wisdom to make us proud? Do you want your children to be popular with the world and have prestige? If they are pushed toward worldly things, the world will catch them and destroy their lives. Do we want them to grow up and become missionaries or evangelists? Do we want them to win a gold crown in the Christian Olympics? Think about some of these questions and what your goals are for your children. Strategies have to be developed to reach those goals.

Parenting is so scarce today that even the world recognizes that parenting is not being done. They realize that parents can help their children stay away from drugs. The Office of National Drug Control Policy (ONDCP) and the Partnership for a Drug-Free America sponsor the National Youth Anti- Drug Media Campaign. They have a gallery of ads for television and radio, and also print and banner ads. Some of the ads are geared directly to parents. Their slogan is "Parents. The Anti-Drug." Things are pretty bad when the world has to remind parents to know where their own children are at all times or know who their friends are and know what they are doing at all times. It is shameful to say, but their message is for Christian parents too.

Now there are commercials out to remind parents to make dinner and have their family sit down and eat together, because in "families that eat dinner together, their children are less likely to do drugs." Most Christian parents are parenting like the world does. As a result, Christian children are also on drugs, having premarital sex, getting pregnant, having abortions, dropping out of school, and doing other things to destroy their lives.

Twofold Training

Christian parent(s) have a twofold discipline and training in the Christian Olympics, for themselves and for their children. The Bible says to "train up a child in the way he should go: and when he is old, he will not depart from it" (Prov. 22:6). Since many children are not being trained, they have nothing to depart from when they are older. They are acting out their lack of discipline and training.

Sometimes problems occur when children become

teenagers, because parent(s) feel that they are grown up and they can now train themselves. That is the worst time to let them go. They now have new feelings to deal with. With their hormones raging and peer pressures, they need parental guidance more than ever. Maybe their hormones are so strong that it overpowers what they were taught before they became teens. It may have caused them to forget. Or maybe, up to that point, they had never been challenged to be disobedient. And finally, they may never have had the opportunity to practice what they had been taught, or they think they are grown now and they just want to challenge parental authority. At this stage in their lives, the wrong decisions that they are allowed to make will follow them into adulthood and affect their Christian race.

The parent(s)' strategy for children is **parental authority.** With this strategy parent(s) can prevent their children from destroying their own lives.

Parent(s) have been given the authority over their children by God. Sometimes parent(s) don't realize the power they have. That means we can get children to do whatever we tell them or want them to do. Some of you may be saying (at least I hope you are saying), "You mean I can make my child [or my children] behave?"

I am so happy to answer yes, yes, yes! Parent(s) have the ability to exercise their God-given control over their children. As long as they are under your roof, they must do what you say. For example, it is not left up to them whether or not they want to attend Sunday school and church. Parent(s) are to make them attend. Sometimes when parent(s) exercise their parental authority, children will try to make their parent(s) feel guilty for being parent(s). Some children will act as though they hate their parent(s), pretend that other parent(s) are better than theirs, try to get their parent(s) to be at odds with each other, and use schemes to break their parent(s)' will in order to get what they want. As a result, parent(s) try to gain popularity with their children and begin to compete for their affection by giving in to their demands.

Once this is accomplished, parent(s) are no longer in control; the children are. All of this is a trick of the devil, influencing children to rebel against parental authority so the parent(s) will give in and so they can destroy their lives before they reach adulthood. Don't allow Satan to use your children to take away the authority God has given you. Can you see the struggle and the wrestling? This is how Satan competes with you—through your children.

The Scriptures teach that parent(s) have an awesome responsibility to keep and do God's commandments, to teach them diligently to their children, to talk of them when sitting down in the house, when walking by the way, and when lying down and rising up (see Deut. 6:1–8). What we learn from these passages is that parent(s) have the responsibility not only to keep God's commandments but also to make sure their children keep them.

For example, children are required by law to attend school to get an education. Parent(s) are obeying God when they obey the law and see to it that their children are properly educated. It is the parent(s)' responsibility to make sure that their children, no matter what age they are, attend all classes and complete all assignments. Parent(s) have to check their homework and make sure they study and are prepared for tests. It is not up to the children to decide whether or not they want to do their assignments; it is the parent(s)' responsibility to make them do it, to keep them from dropping out of school, and to make sure they graduate.

Strategies to Help Children Avoid Pre-Marital Sex

Another problem, even among Christian children, I am sad to say, is pre-marital sex. According to news reports, not only are pre-teens and teenagers involved in pre-marital sex but also children who are still in grade school. God calls this the sin of fornication (1 Cor. 6:18). Some of the devastating effects of fornication are promiscuity, pregnancies, abortions, sexually transmitted diseases, heartaches, depression, drugs, and so on and so on.

Some may be asking how this sin can be avoided (at least I hope you want to know how). Pre-marital sex among children can be avoided first of all by **choosing the friends your children** have. Your children should have friends whose parent(s) have the same biblical Christian values you have. Children whose parent(s) don't approve of fornication will be less likely to commit it.

Doing this is not enough. Even though their friends are Christians, they need to be around adults at all times. They should have an adult as a chaperone when they are home or on any outings away from home. Many times parent(s) think they do not have to watch their children when they are with other Christian children, when they are with the deacon's son or the pastor's daughter. How many times has it happened that the deacon's son impregnated one of the girls in the youth choir? Or the usher's son impregnated the pastor's daughter?

Most children will act the same way when no adults are around, because hormones are domineering and are no respecter of persons. Hormones do not care who they are, where they are, and what they are doing; hormones want what they want and when they want it. It's the same way we were when we were teens; if we did not have parental control or self-control, we did whatever our hormones told us to do. We know now that we have to exercise self-control to keep from committing sexual sins. In fact, self-control is something we will have to practice for the rest of our lives.

The Bible teaches that fornication can be avoided, as well as all the devastating effects resulting from it. Here is how: this is found in 1 Corinthians 7:2, and it is for each man to have his own wife and for each woman to have her own husband, which is marriage. Yes, marriage. I can hear what you maybe saying: "They are just kids; they can't get married," and you are so right. They still need parenting; they have no job and have no place to live. They have not finished school yet. So since they are not mature enough to get married, parent(s) have to try to use discipline and strategies to keep them virgins until they are mature enough to get married.

At all cost, try to keep your children from having intimate relationships with members of the opposite sex. Once they do, it will become extremely hard for them to be kept apart. So the safest thing to do is not to allow dating or courtship for your children until they are mature enough to get married. The intimacy of dating and courting is very intense, which every adult knows. Spending intimate moments regularly with members of the opposite sex will only move them closer and closer through the stages of intimacy. During the final stages of intimacy, if they cannot get married, then it will lead them to have sex outside of marriage and committing the sin of fornication.

This is what happens over and over again. One day they will go a little too far in their affection toward their boyfriend or girlfriend, and before you know it, they are having sex. No matter how good they were, their feelings just took over. Just being a Christian does not help a girl and boy alone who are kissing and hugging each other from having sex.

The strategy is to watch and restrain children so they are not allowed to become so emotionally and physically attached to the opposite sex. In the old days, maybe before many of us were born, parent(s) and other family members, neighbors, and even the whole community would keep a watchful eye on the teenagers. When they saw a boy and girl get too attached to one another they would separate them and keep them apart. Sometimes they would have to send them out of town to another relative.

All of this effort was meant to avoid the inevitable—fornication and pregnancy, which would become the final result if parent(s) allowed their children to start dating and courting before they were mature enough for marriage. They need parental guidance to keep them from getting too intimate too soon with the opposite sex.

Have you ever heard your grandparents or great grandparents tell how they courted? Or have you seen how they courted from movies you've watched about the "good old days"? In those days they married in their early teens. The young teenage boy would visit his young teenage girlfriend's house; it was never the other way around. When he got there, not only was his girlfriend waiting, but so were her parent(s). They were never left alone; in fact, they could not even sit together side by side, because one of her parent(s) would sit between them. This would go on and on until they were married. Those parent(s) were persistent and never let down their guard; they knew what was at stake and what the consequences would be if they didn't take control of the situation.

Parent(s) have the authority to take control of their children's virginity, which is another strategy. It is not up to the children to give it away. According to 1 Corinthians 7:36–38, the father decides (if not the father, then the mother) when his daughter will give away her virginity in marriage. Of course that applies to the male also, because she would marry a male virgin. The male had to wait to give away his virginity until the girl's father gave her in marriage. So in essence, when the father gave away his daughter's virginity in marriage, he was also giving away the virginity of the male that she was going to marry.

This is a lot of responsibility, with all the sex on television, the Internet, the seductive music and clothing, peer pressure, and other things that children are exposed to today. Parent(s) have to try their best to eliminate as much bad exposure for their children as possible.

I am sure that you have heard on the radio or seen on television an ad about a boy who wants to go to a party where no adults will be present. He becomes angry with his father because he will not allow him to go. The boy tells his father that everyone else is going, but the father is firm in his decision and exercises his authority, even though the things the son says and his reaction to his father were negative and may have hurt his father's feelings. I don't know if the ONDCP and the Partnership for a Drug-Free America who sponsored this ad are Christians, but they agree with the biblical principle that parent(s) have authority over their children. We can take this a little bit further; not only are parent(s) the "anti-drug," **but parent(s) are also their children's protection from pre-marital sex.**

Children will benefit from their parent(s)' protection through discipline in the area of self-control. This will be a virtue that they can take into adulthood until they get married. They will learn early that even though they have sexual desires, they do not have to express them—that it is okay not to express them, that they are not going to die, and that fulfilling the desire can be put on hold.

Children need to understand that the attraction they have for a particular person of the opposite sex will one day go away. This is just a phase they are going through. When they get older, they may not even like the same person anymore, which is why being attracted to someone really means nothing. It's just what it is called—an attraction, a force that draws people together. It can draw the wrong people together or can draw the right people together before it is the right time. Help them to not make a big deal about it and to get over it.

When you get to know your children, you will know if they are mature enough to leave home for college. If you see that they are weak-minded, you could have them live at home and commute to a local college. After all, you are paying for their education, and they have to go where you send them. That is another strategy for parent(s)—**protecting their children in the areas where they are weak**.

The strategy also includes parent(s) **teaching their children that their courtship is just being delayed**; it is not something they will never be able to engage in. Then find out what their goals are. Many children just go along with the flow, not having any goals. With no goals, they could become involved in something that they will regret later in life. Help them to figure out a goal, and then help them to achieve it.

To achieve any specific goals, they have to make plans. For example, if their main goal is to get married after they graduate from high school, then they should be working on being prepared spiritually, emotionally, physically, and financially. They can start courting that Christian boy or girl who gave them chills every time they walked by for the past four years (smile), adhering to the principle of pacing the stages of intimacy so that by the time they reach the final stages of intimacy, they will be married.

These strategies are what parent(s) have to try and maintain, especially while their children are living in their homes when they become young adults. If their goal is not to get married right after high school, then their dating and courtship should be delayed until they are ready for marriage. Most girls are ready for marriage, being a wife and mother, after high school, but most boys are not.

Many boys still want to hang out with their friends, be competitive, achieve, and conquer. They may get married, but their hearts are really not in it. So they will get married for the benefits or to give in to personal and outside pressures, but their main goal was to be successful in their careers. Most women will give up their careers for marriage, but most men do not. They will leave their wives and children alone as if they are unmarried in order to climb the ladder of success.

This only leads to what is happening today, and that is this: emotionally, spiritually, and sometimes physically, husbands are not present in the home. This causes wives to begin to feel like widows or divorcees and the children to feel fatherless. Some wives accept this as a part of married life, especially if their husbands keep telling their wives that they are doing it for them and their children or that they are doing God's work, if it involves ministry. (There are ladders of success to climb in Christian organizations, also.)

Then there are the wives who feel so abandoned that they divorce their husbands. Again, as we mentioned earlier about avoiding adultery, if a husband is married to his career or the ministry and is not fulfilling the needs of his wife, that can lead to adultery for both married partners. Once the wife's emotions have shut down, she won't be able to fulfill the needs of her husband, as a result of his abandonment. Sometimes this will drive the husband to another woman or the wife to another man.

This is the strategy that can prevent this from happening: **by parent(s) teaching their boys that if they get married, their primary goal should be to love their wives (Eph. 5:25–33) and be spiritually, emotionally, and physically in the home**. That may mean that they have to give up their career goals and just do whatever job they can do to provide for their families. If they don't feel they can give up their life for a wife, then they should not get married until they do feel that way. They should also practice the strategy of remaining virgins without dating and courtship until they are ready for marriage.

This is one reason why God has given parent(s) the authority to keep their children virgins, because it may be a while before they get married, especially today with so many career and ministry opportunities. It will be easier for them to control themselves sexually if they are virgins. This is why sexual activity before marriage is so devastating; it creates a sexual appetite that only marriage can fill. And it creates a big problem, because now they have to suppress and struggle with their fire of sexual desires until God gives them a mate—or become promiscuous and continue in sin.

Virgins are instructed to avoid fornication by getting married (1 Cor. 7:1). So virgins never have to commit sexual sins. When they become intimately close to the person God wants them to marry, they just have to get married before that intimacy crosses over to fornication. Then what causes virgins to commit fornication and lose their virginity, instead of waiting on God for marriage? Why is it that there are not many virgins today, even in the Christian community? We will answer these important questions later.

Virgins have the desire for sexual intimacy, but since they have never experienced it, they don't have the appetite for it as the married do (1 Cor. 7: 36–38). Some may be wondering: "What about 'it is better to marry than to burn'?" (1 Cor. 7:9). Well, if you look at the context of verse 9, it refers to those who have been married before—the divorced and widows. Paul states in verse 8 that it would be good if they "remain" as they are, like him. We know from this verse that Paul was not a virgin. He was comparing himself to those who have been married before, like him.

The Bible does not say specifically what happened to his marriage. But he was able to live the rest of his life without a spouse. So he was telling those who are no longer married that if they cannot contain (to have inward power, according to the Greek meaning), then they should marry rather than to be on fire with sexual desires. Some people can be married once like Paul and live the rest of their lives unmarried, and some cannot. Also, when Paul wants to address the virgins specifically, he says so, as he does further on in the same chapter.

The Christian Olympics

Therefore, "better to marry than to burn" is not speaking to virgins. This text teaches that the natural sexual desires of virgins are not on fire like those who are or have been married. For example, it's just like something you never ate before. It looks, smells, and feels good, but you have to taste and eat it to acquire an appetite for it.

Now we can answer the important questions that we asked earlier. What causes virgins to commit fornication and lose their virginity instead of waiting on God for marriage? Why is it that there are not many virgins today, even in the Christian community? The Bible speaks of the community of the virgins, the married, the widows, and the divorced. The largest of the four were the married and the virgins, because there were very few widows and divorcees during that time. In the Christian community today, we have the never-married, the married, the divorced, and the widows.

There are no communities of adult virgins today. What I mean is that there are not enough to count as a group to be categorized as such. There are not enough to be studied or included in statistical data. For example, all medical research for adults is for married or sexually active unmarried adults. The reasons why there are very few virgin adults are because most have either gotten married or have become immoral.

The never-marrieds are not called virgins anymore. Immorality has caused the category of virgins to be extinct. The new name for the never-married is singles. This category includes adults who have had marital sexual experiences but now are divorced or widowed, as well as those who have had sexual experiences outside of the bonds of marriage. Therefore the world and the Christian community have defined "singles" as anyone who has never been married or who was but no longer is now.

There are not many virgins in the Christian community today because virginity is not encouraged. In essence, the church does not teach the benefits of virginity over marriage. God has specific purposes for the role of virgins just as He has for married couples. Earlier, we looked briefly at the roles of husbands, wives, and parents. We saw that marriage and the home comes before anything else, even serving the Lord; it must be a couple's utmost priority. The roles of virgins are outlined in 1 Corinthians 7:25–38. In fact, in these passages there are comparisons of virginity and marriage; we can choose one or the other, because we cannot have both roles.

According to these verses, virgins are the community that can serve the Lord without distractions or pursue careers and climb the corporate ladder without the marriage and family distractions. They can also have vocations or ministries that cause them to travel away from home, because they don't have to care for a family. They can stay in church twenty-four hours a day without ever going home. They are the evangelists who travel alone for six months winning souls and the preachers who leave home alone for a week to preach revivals. They are without care of the responsibilities of marriages and families.

These Scriptures are not taught in the Christian community. That is why these two roles are dysfunctional; the married are living as if they are not married, and the virgins are trying to live as if they are married. Since the married are living as if they are not married, the virgins cannot see the significance in their roles, thereby preventing them from seeing God's purpose for their virginity. This is what causes them to lose hope and become immoral.

Some become so discouraged that they get married outside of God's will, and some have divorced. The married must begin to fulfill their own marital roles so that virgins who are now being born or are now growing up to become older adults will begin to see their significant, God-given roles for His purposes so there can be a community of virgins, just as it was in the Bible, to complete the specific missions that they can only accomplish in that state as they are running in the Christian Olympics.

Strategies for Children

Perhaps strategies for children should be added at this point, in case they read this book. Children, God wants you to "...obey your parents in the Lord, for this is right." (Eph. 6:1). Your strategy is to obey your parents. God has made things easy for you. All of the problems and fears of growing up are not for you to worry about. You don't have to figure things out or understand everything. All you have to do is obey God by obeying your parents. He has entrusted them to look out for your best interests, to protect and shield you from the hurtful things in this life.

God also adds a promise to His commandment, that if you honor your father and mother, which means to respect them as superior to you, "it may be well with thee, and thou mayest live long on the earth." (Eph. 6:3). Verse two adds something extra; it's the first commandment with a promise. Have you ever heard of the Ten Commandments? They are a list of God's laws that He wants us to obey. Of all of the commandments that were given, the one for you, to honor your father and mother, was the first that He attached a promise to. In other words He will reward you. All of the other commandments do not have a promise; we are told by God just to "keep them" because God says so. The promise is that if you honor your parents, things will go well for you and you will live a long life on the earth. You may not like what your parents tell you to do or agree with how they discipline you. Maybe you get angry with them because there are certain things that they do not allow you to do that other children are allowed to do. But if you strategize to obey and honor them, you are promised a victorious run in the Christian race.

Strategies for Singles

Those who are not married for whatever reason can develop strategies to avoid yielding to sexual temptations by first knowing God's purpose for singleness.

In 1 Corinthians 7, the apostle Paul's main argument to the virgins, the never-married, the divorced, and widows is that it is better to remain unmarried. The married see the benefits of remaining unmarried, but sometimes singles do not. The benefits are these: you will have fewer problems, you only have to be concerned about taking care of yourself, and you have no distractions. So many married people wish that they did not have to carry the weight of their whole families on their shoulders. There are enough pressures in this world than to have to bear those that come with marriage.

Being single means you can come and go as you please; you don't have to answer to anyone. You can make your own decisions without consulting with anyone. Those who are married have to consult with their families, because whatever decisions they make affect the whole family. In other words, the single life is supposed to be the carefree life. Single men do not have to act like husbands to other women. Single women don't have act like wives to other men. They are totally free from marital duties.

Do you know why God has allowed this privilege of a carefree single life? The reason is so you will be able to sit at Jesus' feet without any distractions (see 1 Cor. 7:35). Singles can spend all day and night with Jesus alone. According to the Scriptures, singles can have an undistracted devotion to the Lord that the married cannot have.

Let's look at the difference between two singles, Martha and Mary. Luke 10:38–42 tells us about a time when Jesus was invited to the home of Martha, who had a sister named Mary. While Mary sat at the feet of Jesus to hear His Word, Martha was distracted with serving and asked Jesus if He didn't care that her sister had left her to do the serving alone. She was saying to Jesus, "Don't you care about me? I am left here alone to do everything by myself. I need help; tell Mary to come and help me."

On the surface it seemed like a reasonable request. Martha had a guest, and she needed help from Mary to serve the guest. But Martha was so distracted that she did not care what Mary was doing; she wanted her to be distracted with serving as she was. All Martha could see was that she was left alone to serve by herself. Jesus can settle the disagreements and disputes in our relationships; just look at how Jesus handles this. Jesus does not tell Mary to go and help her sister, Martha, as we would expect Him or her brother or mother or father to say. He tells Martha that she has become distracted and agitated about many things that are not necessary.

In other words, her priorities were in the wrong place, and because of that she is disturbed. She does not need to become a distraction to Mary to keep her from hearing God's Word. And she does not need to get Mary distracted just because she is distracted. Jesus tells her that what Mary has chosen to do, to sit at His feet and hear His Word, is the good part, and He will not take that away from her. Jesus was saying that it is better for Mary to hear His Word than to help Martha serve. It is better to sit at the feet of Jesus than to be distracted with many things.

The strategy for the single life is to **be without distractions and sit at the feet of Jesus.** Jesus does not want singles to let their lives get so distracted that they cannot sit at the feet of Jesus. Martha was acting like a lot of singles act today—agitated, troubled, disturbed, stressed, and worried about things that only distract them from God's purposes and the benefits of being carefree singles, to listen to Jesus and sit at His feet.

If you were married, you could not have an undistracted devotion to the Lord. Your purpose as a single, however, is not to keep yourself busy with other people's matters or to give yourself to everyone because you don't have a mate. Those are the biggest traps singles fall into, because they become so weary like Martha, filling their lives with things to keep them busy to the point that being single becomes burdensome. This can cause discouragement and lead singles into immorality. Instead, God wants singles to find their fulfillment in His specific ministry for their lives. The purpose for singleness is being with Jesus without distractions, which is a privilege the married do not have.

Single parents can also take advantage of this strategy. Though they do not have a spouse to distract them, they do have a child or children. But the time they would ordinarily spend with a spouse becomes a God-given opportunity to have undistracted devotion to Him.

Whether you have never been married, widowed, or divorced, it's best to take advantage of these privileges now before you get married according to God's will, because once you do, you will no longer have that privilege. God's love and divine wisdom wants to spare you of all the trouble of the married life (1 Cor. 7:28). According to 1 Corinthian 7:35, God is not against you. He's not trying to withhold something good from you (Ps. 84:11). He has allowed you to be single for your advantage; your singleness is designed to help you.

Once you realize this it will help you in the area of yielding to sexual temptations—because you have someone to be intimate with, and that person is Jesus Christ (1 Cor. 6:13). This statement sums up what God is saying to you: **Being single means that Jesus Christ is enough for you; you don't need another person to complete your life**. If you could grab hold of this statement and begin to believe it, you will be so content that it will no longer matter to you whether you get married or not.

To avoid sexual immorality, which is to have sexual

relations with someone who is not your husband or wife, for the single is to **flee**, according to 1 Corinthians 6:18. Knowing that God is not depriving you of marriage but is looking out for what is best for you will help you to develop a strategy to flee fornication. Now you can see why you don't need to be distracted—so you can sit at Jesus' feet and hear His Word. Being distracted with the wrong things can cause you to become immoral.

The avoidance of spending time alone with the opposite sex is one of the best strategies you can have. Even if you are tempted to commit fornication you cannot yield to that temptation unless both you and your friend are alone. Most of the time you have to get to know a person before you develop intimacy with them, so avoid becoming intimate with a member of the opposite sex. When you meet someone who shares the same values that you have, seek God to see if you should begin a relationship. Remember, your goal in a relationship should be marriage. If you both have the same goals, then slowly pace your stages of intimacy. If God is leading you to marriage, by the time you are near the closing stages of intimacy you will have avoided fornication by getting married.

Until that time you will be practicing sexual abstinence, which even the married do from time to time. In this chapter we discussed the scriptures that explain why married people abstain or give up sexual relations to fast and pray together, for an agreed-upon time. But they cannot do it for long because their competitor, Satan, will tempt them since they do not have self-restraint. But singles can go on continuously giving up sex in favor of fasting, praying, and seeking God without the distraction of sex. How much more time singles can devote to the Lord than those who are married!

Today many married couples practice sexual abstinence on a regular basis (without God's stipulation in 1 Cor. 7:5) as if they were single. They see the advantages of it, as when the wife takes her vacation one month and her husband takes his the following month. This way both of them will not miss work in the same month. They will have to practice sexual abstinence for two months. Sometimes spouses have projects they are working on, and they need a long time with no distractions to work on it, so one spouse will go away leaving the other spouse at home. They will practice sexual abstinence for as long as it takes in order to complete their projects.

Many athletes are separated from their wives during the playing season. Especially during championship games, their wives stay in a separate hotel from them because their husbands have to stay with the team. They give up sex to keep them from being distracted from the game. Many military couples are separated from each other; some have to practice sexual abstinence for many years. They cannot take their spouses everywhere the military sends them. And even if they could, especially during times of war, the military does not want them to be distracted by sexual relations with their spouses. Sexual abstinence is giving up a desire of the flesh to achieve something far greater that otherwise you would not be able to achieve. It's a privilege and a virtue for singles only, so maximize it and take advantage of it.

In conclusion, let us lay down our heavy burdens and the sin surrounding us. Let's not start things that could become habit-forming, and let's avoid sins that we do not have to commit.

CHAPTER 5

The Competitions

Now that we are not carrying heavy loads of weight and sin while we are trying to run, we will be able to endure the race.
"...let us run with patience the race that is set before us," (Heb. 12:1). Before we discuss the competitions, we will look at the correct attire we must wear, just like the athletes in the Olympic Games.

Part 1
Getting Equipped
Attire: What We Wear
Those who compete in the Olympic Games wear attire appropriate for their particular sport. The boxers wear boxing attire, runners wear running attire and so forth. It becomes extremely hard sometimes to look at some of the sporting events because of the uniforms they wear. What I mean is that some are too tight and too short. Men and women show too much of their private body parts. In some cases, the men have on more clothes than the women.

As spectacles in the Christian Olympics, we must be careful not to wear anything or do anything that will cause our fellow spectacles to stumble while running in the Christian race (see Rom. 14:21). Have you ever watched children play or run in a race and then somebody puts something in front of them to make them trip and fall? That fall makes them stop running. If they are not seriously hurt they can get back up and continue to run, but it made them lose too much time. Now it's hard to gain the distance they lost. If they are seriously hurt, they have to stop running until they heal. Sometimes the injury is permanent, and they will never be able to run again.

This is what Romans 14: 21 teaches us: to not do or say anything to cause another spectacle to stumble. We have to deny ourselves even of something that we like if it would cause another Christian to become weak in their Christian walk. It's the same way with the way we dress; we should never wear something that reveals parts of our bodies that should be left to the imagination or that should be restricted to the privacy of our own homes.

Then there are some things that are neither right nor wrong but are offensive to some but for others are not offensive. For example, some churches may quarrel over whether or not the pastor should wear a robe when he preaches. Since there are no scriptures that can solve the dispute, then how can it be solved? Using this scripture in Romans, if it would be offensive to some for the pastor to preach without a robe, then the main priority is not to offend. The resolution for the dispute is to have the pastor wear a robe to keep from offending anyone. Because a robe is not an offensive garment, it should not offend anyone if the pastor wears it.

According to James 3, we must also be careful not to offend one another with the things that we say. The verses in this chapter go on to explain how the tongue is such a small member of the body, but it is the hardest to control. If the tongue is controlled, then the whole body will be also. This small member of the body can do more damage than any other member of the body.

I'm sure you can remember a time when someone said something to you that hurt your feelings. Even if he apologized, you still felt the hurt. It was as if someone punched you, but the pain of a physical punch would have eventually gone away. It's not so with the tongue; the pain may hurt for years or for a lifetime, because what we hear goes into our minds like a tape recorder on replay. It will replay it over and over again, no matter how much we try to forget it. The devil knows just when to replay it in our minds, to make it sound as if we are hearing it for the first time.

Just while we are praying or reading the Bible, or right after someone's tongue gave you a double whammy (that's a hurting word, back-to-back). It may not just hurt, but it also may affect the decisions that we make, the things that we do, and the places where we go. But most devastating of all is the effect it may have on our relationship to God. Many times when we are hurt, we are too discouraged to communicate with God. This is the time we need God the most, because only He can make the replay sound dull to our hearing and heal what is hurting us. We should at all cost refrain from doing anything, wearing anything, or saying anything that will make our fellow spectacles stumble and fall while running in the Christian Olympics.

The Whole Armor of God

During the ancient Olympic Games, there were contests that involved racing in armor. I am sure you have seen movies portraying the ancient times with men in the arena racing with their armor on. Well, that is similar to the attire or the uniform that the spectacles wear in the Christian Olympics—the whole armor of God, found in Ephesians 6:11–18. The only clothing we wear, other than the non-offensive clothing that we spoke about earlier, is the whole armor of God. This armor is not a heavy metal like the armor worn during ancient times. It is very light. As a matter of fact, we cannot even see or feel it, because it is spiritual.

Remember who our competitors are: the world, the flesh, and the devil. Therefore, our attire has to be divinely suited for spiritual competition. The whole armor of God consists of the girdle of truth, the breastplate of righteousness, the shoes of the gospel of peace, the shield of faith, the helmet of salvation, and the sword of the Spirit.

The **girdle of truth** is like a belt that goes around the waist, in order to carry our offensive weapon with us. Whatever is carried on this belt is Truth and is used for carrying the **sword of the Spirit**, which is the Word of God. It is the only weapon that we have to fight with. Listen to how Hebrews 4:12 describes this weapon: "For the word of God is quick, and powerful, and sharper than any two-edged sword, piercing even to the dividing asunder of soul and spirit, and of the joints and marrow, and is a discerner of the thoughts and intents of the heart."

Since it is such a powerful weapon, it is imperative that we know how to use it. According to 2 Timothy 2:15, we should know the Word of God like a workman who is not ashamed. A workman who can cut something straight or right will not be ashamed of his work. So it is with the Word of Truth; we have to learn the necessary skills in order to know how to rightly divide it.

In other words, while we are racing in our armor and we have to take out our sword, after the world hits us with its wisdom, we have to know what passages in the Bible to use to fight back or attack with. The rest of the armor of God is defensive, such as **the helmet of salvation**, which gives us assurance of our salvation. It protects our head from our competitors.

Another defensive weapon is the breastplate of righteousness. A breastplate protects the body, so we must put on God's protection of righteousness for our body. Then there are the shoes of the gospel of peace. Everywhere our feet tread we will be ready to defend ourselves with the gospel of peace, Jesus Christ. The shield of faith, another defensive weapon, is used to put out the arrows of fire thrown at us to attack our faith while we are in the race. The arrows of fire are the things that the world says to us: "You're not going to make it" or "I hope you fall." "Don't you want to quit?" or "If you dedicate your life to serving Christ, you will never have anything; you will lose your life." "You will never get married" or "Your spouse will walk away from you."

That is similar to what a heckler or a spectator in the stands would say as they're watching the Olympic Games. They're trying to cause a competitor to lose faith in himself. Can you think of some others right now? What about: "You believe in someone you can't see; how do you know He is even there?" "He was not raised from the dead." "There is no God." When we hold up our shield of faith the arrows will bounce off it, and that will put out the fire. This is our attire from our head to our feet, which makes us fully clothed for the Christian Olympics.

Prayer, Our Breathing Exercises

After we are completely dressed with the whole armor of God, which is spiritual, we pray continuously in the Spirit to God. Praying is communicating to God what we wish for, which means in every season (in the Greek). No matter what it is, we can tell God what we wish for since He is the only one who can make it come true. It will never sound too far-fetched to Him, but if we told someone else, they might think we're crazy. And if our wish does not come true, because we told God we know that it was not His will—and He will give us grace to help us accept His will.

God wants us to pour out to Him in prayer whatever is on our hearts and ask Him anything we want. When you pray and pour out your heart to God, don't you feel better? God has a way of healing us when we pray. The situation may be the same, but because you told God about it, He comforts and strengthens you in the area where you were weak. He gives you encouragement to continue in the race. So just as the athletes do breathing exercises while they are running so they have enough wind, strength, and stamina to continue running, we have to continuously huff and puff prayers as our breathing exercises (Lk.18:1-8; 1 Th.5:17).

Then we are to watch and pray for our fellow spectacles in the competition. Remember what was said earlier, that we are not in competition with each other the way the athletes competing in the Olympic Games are. They are competing against one another, so they are not going to help a fellow competitor win. Since we are all spectacles we are to help one another win.

We are to watch like watchmen and pray to make sure that our fellow spectacles have on their helmet of salvation and their breastplate of righteousness, and that their sword of the Spirit is on their belt of truth. While we are running and a spectacle falls, we are to pick them up and keep running. This will not cause us to lose the race or take longer to get to the finish line, because this is all a part of the Christian race.

Spiritual Gifts

With the whole armor of God on, we are equipped with the necessary attire to compete in the Christian Olympics. Now we have to be equipped with our spiritual gifts. As we mentioned in previous chapters, the Christian race is a running and fighting contest. It is individual; it takes place every day and is a lifetime of faithful service to God. You may be asking: "What do we do in the contest?" "Just what does faithful service to God have to do with it?" To answer these questions we are going to discuss spiritual gifts.

The Christian Olympics

The Christian Olympics began when the Holy Spirit baptized believers(spectacles) of all nationalities into one body, the body of Christ, which meant every believer became a member of the body of Christ. As compared to the human body, Christ is the head and the members of his body are the believers, also called the church or Christians. Just as the parts or members of the human body have many functions, the members of the body of Christ function with the spiritual gifts of each believer. The spiritual gifts are the feet, hands, ears, eyes, nose, and other parts of the body of Christ. Each believer has been placed in the body of Christ according to His will. He has decided whom He wants to be His nose, eyes, ears, feet, hands, and other body parts(1Cor.12:12-27) . Just as there are names for every member of the human body, members of the body of Christ are named according to their spiritual gifts. Here are several lists of the spiritual gifts and offices:

- Word of wisdom, word of knowledge, faith, the gifts of healing, working of miracles, prophecy, discerning of spirits, diverse kinds of tongues, and the interpretation of tongues. (From 1 Cor. 12:8–10)
- Apostles, prophets, teachers, miracles, gifts of healings, helps, governments, and diversities of tongues. (From 1 Cor. 12:28)
- Prophecy, ministry, teaching, exhortation, giving, ruling, and extending mercy. (From Rom. 12:6–8)
- Apostles, prophets, evangelists, pastors and teachers. (From Eph. 4:11)

The above lists of the members of the body of Christ describe their function or service in the body. (Not all of the gifts in the above lists operate today the same as they did in the early stages of the authentication of the church age.) These spiritual gifts enable us to serve God in the specific capacity He has designed for us. Believers have to find out what their spiritual gifts are and how they were placed in the body. It is not something that we can pick or choose. Once we find out what they are through the guidance of the Holy Spirit, then that is the capacity in which we are to serve God faithfully in the Christian race. These are the supernatural abilities that equip spectacles to function in various competitions in the Christian Olympics. Just as athletes have special talents and abilities to function in their particular sport in the Olympic games.

The problem today (and in the Corinthian church in the first century) is that many of us want to choose our own gifts or we want the gift someone else has. God distributes the gifts according to His own will. Many Christians think everyone should have the same gifts. Paul explains to them that a body has many members; if the whole body was an eye, then how could there be hearing? How could there be a body? That is why there are many members but one body. We can never say that one spiritual gift is needed more or is more important than another one is.

With our spiritual gifts, there should be no division among us. We are to treat one another the same and have the same care for each other. Just as in the human body, when one member is hurt, the whole body hurts. When the member is healed, the whole body feels better. When a member does well, all of the members rejoice with that member. So it should be with the body of Christ. Once we know what our gifts are, then we must rely on the Holy Spirit to place us where He wants to use our gifts.

The church is becoming more and more dysfunctional. Many Christians do not know what their spiritual gifts are, even those who hold offices like deacons or ministers' wives. Some do not use their gifts, and some churches will only use the gifts that they feel are important. Some are following after gifts that belong to someone else. "If he can do that, so can I," they say, or "If she can go there, then I'll become what she is and go there too"—never stopping to ask, "What does God want me to do?"

If you don't use the gift that God gave you, the body cannot function properly. Some preachers preach the way someone else does. If they have the gift to preach, then God has given them a unique style of preaching (1 Cor. 12:4–7). Many preachers become pastors without having the spiritual gifts of pastors and teachers. This is why so many preachers leave the ministry or fall into sin; God has not gifted them for that office.

When we have an office or position that we are not gifted to do, then the body of Christ cannot be edified. Nor can the body function properly if we don't use our gifts where God wants us to use them (Eph. 4:10–13). Some people choose churches or ministries because that is where everyone goes. Some may say, "My family has been members here for years and years" - "My friends are here" - "I'm only here because of the choir and the music" -"The preacher makes me feel good; he gives me chills" - "It's the largest church" - "They pay their staff well" - "It will look good on my resume" - "Being a member [or having this position] will give me prestige." None of these reasons are an excuse for not obeying God's call to the place and ministry where He wants us to serve.

For an example of spectacles who used their unique spiritual gifts where God wanted them to use them, first we will meet Philip the Evangelist. Since he was honest and full of the Holy Ghost and wisdom, he was one of the seven men who were chosen to be deacons by the apostles. He probably had the spiritual gifts of ministry and evangelism. The gift of ministry means to serve; by having the office of a deacon he was able to serve the people of God. With his gift of evangelism, he went to Samaria and preached Christ and led Samaria and even Simon, a sorcerer, to Christ. The apostles heard about all this while they were in Jerusalem and sent Peter and John to join him (Acts 8:4–25).

After an evangelistic meeting of preaching Christ to the multitudes, the angel of the Lord called Philip away from the crowd and told him to arise and go to Gaza and also told him how to get there. He was not told why but he left Samaria and did exactly what he was told. When he got there, he met a man from Ethiopia who was an official for the Ethiopian queen. He was returning from worshiping in Jerusalem and was sitting in his chariot reading Isaiah 53:7–8.

Then the Holy Spirit told Philip to go over to the Ethiopian and get into his chariot. The Ethiopian could not understand what he was reading. Philip explained that passage while using the opportunity to preach Christ to him from the same scriptures. (A person with the gift of evangelism can take any scripture and preach the good news of Jesus Christ. From Genesis to Revelation, they can see the gospel.) Philip led the Ethiopian to Christ and baptized him. Immediately afterwards, the Holy Spirit sent him to preach in other cities. Philip the Evangelist knew what his gifts were, and he used them faithfully. He allowed God to put him where He wanted him to serve, as he ran on his racetrack and he possessed the gifts for the offices he held (Acts 8:26–40).

You don't hear too much today about the office of an evangelist that Philip held, but there are many preachers and pastors even though God is still giving the gift of evangelism and the office of an evangelist. Many preachers are waiting to become pastors; they should check to see if they have the gift of an evangelist. Many pastors may have misunderstood their gifts and should be evangelists instead.

Now let us meet Deaconess Phoebe (Rom. 16:1–2), who served at the church of Cenchrea near Corinth. She had the spiritual gift of ministry, which means serving. The apostle Paul spoke highly of her to the church in Rome because she was on her way there to take care of some business.

The Christian Olympics

Paul told the church in Rome to receive her in the Lord and to assist her in whatever she needed from them. She may have had the gift of governments, which means to steer, pilot, or direct, being an administrator in church affairs.

Paul goes on to point out something else about her, that she was a protector of others and himself. Phoebe held the right office in the church as a deaconess, since a deaconess's duty was to serve and she had the spiritual gift of serving. As a deaconess, she was also able to serve the church with another gift, that of government or administration as she ran on her racetrack.

Meet Priscilla and Aquila (Rom. 16:3–5), a married couple whom the apostle Paul calls his helpers. Both of them had the spiritual gifts of helping, and together they helped Paul. They helped fellow believers by allowing the church to meet in their own home. Paul told the church in Rome how they risked their necks for his life. Not only is he thankful for that, but so were all of the churches of the Gentiles. When Paul met them in Corinth, he stayed with them because they had the same skill he had—tent-making—and he worked with them.

You don't see this often, but according to Acts 18:3 both Priscilla and Aquila made tents. Later they traveled with Paul to Ephesus. While in Ephesus, we see another of their gifts in operation. Apollos (Acts 18:24–28), who was eloquent and mighty in the scriptures, was speaking and teaching, using his gifts. But he only knew of the baptism of John. When Aquila and Priscilla heard him, they were able to teach him the way of God so he could teach more accurately. Wow—this couple was truly a team! Not only did they have the same occupation and the gift of helps, but both of them had the gift of teaching too, and utilized them as they ran on their racetracks.

A final point: let us learn an important lesson from

athletes and their talents and abilities. Those who have the skills to jump are not going to compete in the Olympic Games as tennis players. Though they may like tennis, their best skills are in jumping. They know that they could never win the gold in the tennis competition. Neither would those who are skilled in boxing try to compete as runners just because they think they could do it or because their friends are runners. They know they can only compete in the sport they are skilled and talented in. In some cases, that may involve more than one skill. Swimmers are not going to compete in basketball simply because of the prestige that goes along with being basketball players.

Athletes know what their abilities and talents are and will train and only in those skills in order to compete in the Olympic Games. It is the same in the Christian Olympics; we have to be like the athletes, we can only compete effectively if we train and utilize our own God-given abilities called spiritual gifts that we are supernaturally equipped with. We must use them where and when God wants us to use them to compete and win the gold crowns.

Part 2
Let the Games Begin!

Running in the Race

Once we know our spiritual gifts, this brings us to how we run and fight with them. With our spiritual gifts and spiritual attire on we are equipped for the competitions. The competitions are **in *running, hurdling, boxing, fighting with wild beasts, and wrestling*.**

All runners in the Olympic Games run on racetracks in a huge stadium before millions of spectators. Each runner runs in his or her own lane. It is the same in the Christian Olympics, only the stadium is much bigger because it encompasses the whole world. All the spectacles in this worldwide stadium run using their spiritual gifts in their individual lane. In the Olympic Games, the runners run in the marathon for several hours and the race is over, but in the Christian Olympics the race goes on for days, months, years, and decades.

It's a lifetime of running on our own individual track in the world. St. Paul was able to say that he finished his course (Acts 20:24; 2 Tim. 4:7), which meant his race, his individual track, at the end of his life. That meant he used his spiritual gifts and did what God called him to do. He knew without a shadow of doubt that he had been obedient, having done all the assignments God asked him to complete up to that point. If you were to die right now would you be able to say that you finished your course? You may be thinking: "You can't say anything if you are dead." You know what I mean; it's just a figure of speech. I'll put it another way—if you knew that you were going to die today, would you be able to say that you finished your course?

I know we all have goals that we have not accomplished yet, but up to this point, where we are right now, if we had lived a life of obedience to Christ, we should be able to say with St. Paul, "I have finished my course"(2 Tim. 4:7). Finishing also means that we stayed in our individual racing lane. If an athlete goes off course into another runner's lane, besides causing a catastrophe, he would be disqualified without finishing the race.

The apostle Paul knew his ministry was to the Gentiles (Rom. 11:13), and he was faithful to his ministry. When you know what your ministry is you stay the course; you stay in your own lane. When the apostle was preaching in the synagogue, he mentioned how John the Baptist fulfilled his course (Acts 13:24–25). When he ran on his racetrack, he was preparing the way before Christ, and he accomplished that.

St. Paul goes on to say in 2 Timothy 4:7, "I have kept the faith," what does he mean that he kept the faith? First, let's look at what "the faith" is. The faith is the Christian faith: which is believing that there is one God who is three persons in one: The Father, The Son, and The Holy Spirit. They created the heaven, the earth, and made man. (Gen.1:1-2,26, Jn.1:1-3,Mt.28:19,1Tim. 2:5)The Son of God became a man and His name is Jesus Christ. He was born of the virgin Mary(Lk.1:35,Mt.1:16,23),was crucified on the cross for the sins of the world, was buried, rose again bodily from the grave(1Cor.15:3-4), then went back to heaven bodily to sit on the right hand of God The Father and is coming back again(Acts 1;9-11,Rom 8:34).This is "the faith" that St. Paul kept, which meant that he continued believing in the faith and never wavered from it. He never allowed anyone to persuade him to believe otherwise. While we are running on our racetracks we have to hold on, be strong, and don't let go of "the faith."

Hurdling

Are you familiar with the hurdles? It's a race in the Olympic Games in which runners have to jump over a barrier while they are running. Sometimes the hurdles are spaced several yards from one another, and then there are some that are only a few feet from each other or are back-to-back.

Nevertheless, the athletes have to keep jumping over them while they are running as if they were not there. They cannot stop and climb over them or go around them; in fact, they do not stop at all. It looks as though they are still running, but when they get to the hurdles they just stretch their legs high and the next thing you know, they are over the barrier. Some jump over the barriers without their legs touching them.

The races in the Christian Olympics are hurdle races. While we are running on our racetracks, barriers of trials and tribulations are put in our way to keep us from finishing the race. Sometimes they are yards apart (several years) or several feet apart (months, weeks, days, or back-to-back). These hurdles are a test of our faith to see if we are going to keep running and jumping and be victorious over our trials. Will we keep running, or will we stop because it is too difficult to jump over the hurdles? We have to do one or the other; either we jump or we stop running, because we can't climb over the hurdles and we can't go around them.

Sometimes our trials and tribulations actually cause us physical and emotional pain, which I call *hurt*les. When we are hurting, the pain can slow us down and cause us to stop running and jumping over our hurdles. God wants us to continue to run and jump, even if we have to do it with teardrops rolling down our faces as we strain and grit our teeth because of our heartaches and pain.

I believe one of the reasons God compares the Christian to an athlete is because of some of the pain, stress, and strain involved in being a Christian. When we suffer for following Christ it sometimes seems strange, and we may wonder what is going on. But when we look at the hard training, workout, suffering, pain, and competition of athletes and compare all that to being spiritual athletes, it gives us a better perspective and understanding of what we are going through.

In hurdling, the barriers are never moved from the track; the runners have to jump or they cannot finish the race. Unlike the Olympic Games where some races are held without hurdles, the races in the Christian Olympics always include hurdles.

We can count on having trials or hurdles while we are running on our racetracks. God wants us to be like the hurdlers while we are running in the Christian race, so that when hurdles are put in front of us on the racetracks, we will jump over them one after the other—jumping high and victoriously—stretching our endurance capability—over the hurdles without touching them, while still running.

Have you ever tried walking or running a long distance and it was very difficult to endure? On the other hand, when you had to endure that same distance again it was a little easier. It did not seem as burdensome. That was because you kept on walking and running to reach your destination, which stretched your endurance capability. When you had to do it again you had already developed the muscle and stamina to go the distance. It is the same way in the Christian race; endurance, patience, and longsuffering help us through our trials and tribulations so we can be stronger and have the capability to endure another trial.

Fighting in the Race

Boxing
In 2 Timothy 4:7, the apostle Paul says, "I have fought a good fight, ..." which introduces us to fighting in the race. In the Olympic Games, the athletes who where running did not have to fight while they were running in the race. But in the Christian Olympics, the spectacles have to run and fight at the same time. Our fight is "...the good fight of faith,..." (1 Tim. 6:12). It's a good fight because it is for a good cause, a fight of faith in our belief in the Good News of the Gospel of Jesus Christ.

Sometimes we have to publicly defend what we believe, we have to hold on to our beliefs no matter what those who oppose us are saying. Paul referred to the fighting race as boxing in 1 Corinthians 9:26; the meaning of the Greek word for fight means to box. There's a technique in boxing called jabbing, which is a punch with short, straight blows. When we are witnessing to the cults—while we are running on the racetracks and they say they don't believe in the gospel— we jab them with Romans 1:16. Then when they say they don't believe in hell, we give them a double jab, with Luke 16:19–31; that's like a right and left hand punch, one right after the other. It's so quick that it looks as if the jabs struck simultaneously.

Fighting with Wild Beasts

The apostle Paul saw the beast fights during his visit to Rome, and he compared them to the fight he had in Ephesus. He mentions in 1 Cor. 15:32 that he fought with a beast, which meant in the Greek to fight with a wild beast. To get a better understanding of what Paul was speaking about, let's look at what actually happened in Ephesus. The full account of what happened is found in Acts 19:23–41.

Paul was preaching as he was running on his racetrack in Ephesus for about three years. During this time, everyone who lived in Asia heard the Word of the Lord Jesus, to the extent that the Word of God grew mightily and prevailed, and many believed. (Acts 19:1–20). Ephesus was a capital city and had a temple of the goddess Diana, known as one of the Seven Wonders of the World. Many were persuaded by Paul to leave their idol worship of Diana—to serve the living and true God, Jesus Christ. But this caused a problem with a silversmith named Demetrius, because he made silver shrines of Diana and made a profit from selling them. He called a meeting with others who had the same craft and also profited from making shrines to Diana to tell them that Paul's preaching was jeopardizing their livelihood by telling people that gods made with hands are no gods at all.

Out of all the crafts they made, most of their wealth probably came from silver shrines that they made of the goddess Diana. Demetrius incited them more by saying that not only did this make their craft useless but also the temple wouldn't mean anything and the greatness of Diana, whom everyone worshiped, would be destroyed. The craftsmen became full of wrath and started shouting praises to the goddess Diana. Then the whole city was filled with confusion and was in an uproar. Two of Paul's travel companions were suddenly snatched away together and violently rushed into the theater (this was so ironic, because theaters were where spectacles were exhibited). The apostle Paul wanted to go into the theater, but the disciples and some of the officials of Asia pleaded with him not to. Alexander wanted to address the crowd, and they rejected him and shouted praises to the goddess Diana for two hours. It took the town clerk to quiet the people down by reasoning with them to keep them from doing something rash. He dismissed the crowd.

This is what Paul was referring to: the uproar of enemies of the cross of Christ in Ephesus was just like fighting with wild beasts. Imagine a group of missionaries whose mission was to go to a city where there were many drug dealers. Most of the people in the city were saved through the missionaries witnessing to them, causing the drug dealers to lose a lot of business. You can imagine what the dealers would try to do to those missionaries. Or maybe it's the state liquor stores in our neighborhoods; we could stand near them and hand out salvation tracts, which would cause them to lose business. The owners would be furious, and there would be no telling what they would do to us.

This is one of the main reasons why Christians are persecuted today; it's because of wealth. When people become Christians they stop their idol worshiping (things made with hands), things they thought that they could not live without. They suddenly find that they don't need them any longer. They now serve the living God, who has replaced their idols. Since there are profits in idol worship, their merchants lose money and they attack those who worship the true and living God.

In the Christian Olympics we are running on our racetracks fighting against wild beasts. There are many instances where spectacles have been killed in the worldwide stadium just as in some of the beast fights in Rome, in which the athlete competed against a beast and the beast killed him.

Stephen was one of the first deacons chosen by the apostles. He spoke with so much wisdom that in certain synagogues lies were made up about him. When he addressed the charges, the people were so convicted by God's Word that they covered their ears, grabbed him, threw him out of the city, and stoned him to death (Acts 6:8–7:60).

Have you ever given someone God's Word and they got so angry with you that they wanted to physically hurt you? Or maybe you actually got into a physical fight for the cause of Christ; that is fighting with a wild beast. In many countries where Christianity is forbidden, Christian churches undergo persecution regularly. Their fight with wild beasts sometimes causes them to lose their lives.

These are just some examples of God's servants who had the ability to use God's Word to pierce hearts like a two-edged sword.

Wrestling

In the Christian Olympics we are running on our racetracks, jumping over hurdles, boxing, and occasionally fighting with beasts. We also wrestle. If you ever watched a wrestling match you know that it is not the type of sport where two opponents in the match use their fists to fight as in boxing. Instead, the opponents use their hands while struggling to force their opponents to the ground.

It is the same ordeal with wrestling in the Christian Olympics, except we still have to run. While running on the racetrack our competitor struggles with us in order to get us to fall down. The difference is that we do not wrestle with flesh and blood; our fight is against the devil's kingdom and spiritual wickedness. The devil has a kingdom of demons whose job it is to do anything possible to make us fall using their skills of deception, even as we are running on the racetracks.

It was mentioned earlier about the attire that we have to

The Christian Olympics

wear in the Christian Olympics, the whole armor of God. Now we can see why God wants us to run on the racetracks with our armor on. That is the only way we can wrestle with the devil and his demons and still be standing on our feet when the match is over. The Bible says to put on the whole armor of God so that we can stand against the wiles of the devil (Eph. 6:11)—so we can continue to run, leaving the devil and his host on the ground until our next wrestling match.

The Christian Olympics is a spiritual race of spectacles running, jumping over hurdles, boxing, fighting with wild beasts, and wrestling on the racetracks—competing with the devil, the flesh, and the world by utilizing God-given, supernatural skills and abilities like an athlete has, called spiritual gifts. The spectacles put on the spiritual attire that is appropriate for these skills and abilities—the whole armor of God. As we are running on the racetracks of the world we are to keep looking forward to Jesus, because He was our forerunner and He showed us how to run and win. And He will be at the finish line waiting for us at the end of our race. Knowing that we will see Him when we finish helps us to endure the race (Heb. 12:2).

CHAPTER 6

The Suffering

Part 1
Good or Bad?

All athletes who train and compete in the Olympic Games experience various forms of suffering. They suffer physically when they strain or pull a muscle. They have pain in their feet, legs, and lower back or get a cramp, or have shoulder and neck pain. Maybe they will sprain or twist their ankles or tear their ligaments. They may experience severe head trauma or broken limbs. Maybe the suffering is complete exhaustion from constant wear and tear on the body.

Emotional suffering can result when they cannot be with their families, especially for holidays, because they have to travel or train during that time. They may experience loneliness because they have to keep a schedule, be on a strict diet, and practice a disciplined life that others around them do not have to follow. They may have to go to foreign countries to get advanced training or to compete, which can heighten their loneliness; being in strange countries makes them feel like aliens. But all of this is worth it, because they know that it will make them better athletes so they can master their competition and bring home the gold medals. What about the stress of the competition itself—before, during, and afterwards? Finally they may experience the feeling of suffering loss when they don't win the gold or any medals at all.

Throughout the Bible those who followed the true God experienced suffering. Suffering can be result from something bad we have done, which is called chastisement, or for something good we have done, which is called trials, testing, or persecution.

Athletes also suffer when they don't obey their coaches' and trainers' regimens, which were tailored and customized to fit their athletic needs in order to prepare them properly for their competitions. For example, not getting enough sleep or rest the week or night before the competitions could cause them to get tired before the competition ends, making it harder for them to play their particular sport. Poor nutrition, eating the wrong foods, not eating enough, or eating too much can also affect their performances. Not exercising enough, too much exercise, or too little can cause them to suffer tremendous pain during and after the competitions.

It is the same way in the Christian Olympics: if we don't follow our trainer and coach, the Holy Spirit, and abide by His customized plan outlined in the Bible, which is tailored to our needs, we will suffer. God has graciously given us His written Word.

The Old Testament saints were not in the Christian Olympics, but their lives offer us examples of real-life situations to compare to the Christian race or competition.

Chastisement

God gives us the perfect example of suffering as chastisement: when the children of Israel were in the wilderness or desert for forty years and were chastised for their disobedience and unbelief. God had miraculously delivered them from their enemies in Egypt and was in the process of taking them to the Promised Land, Canaan. But they began to disbelieve what God had promised them. When spies were sent out to survey the land, some, like Caleb, came back with a good report stating that it was just as God said it would be. But then other men who went with Caleb believed that the inhabitants they saw there were stronger than they were, so "they brought up an evil report of the land" (Num. 13:32). The congregation began to complain and wish that they had died in Egypt or in the wilderness. They decided to "make a captain" and return to Egypt (Num. 14:4).

Joshua and Caleb pleaded with the people not to rebel against God or fear the people of the land, because God was on their side. But the congregation was so angry that they wanted to stone them. Just before they were getting ready to stone the two men, "…the glory of the LORD appeared in the tabernacle of the congregation before all the children of Israel." (Num. 14:10), which prevented them from exercising their rage.

This was not the first time they complained and did not believe in God's Word and His promises. It started from the time God miraculously delivered them out of the hands of the Egyptians to their journeys in the wilderness. They were able to see what God could do and how He provided for their every need. But they still did not trust God. It is the same way with us sometimes; even though God has delivered us from our enemies in the past we still don't trust Him to take care of us in the present or future. We read God's Word, but we don't believe what we have read.

After God shows us that He is God, then He expects us to increase our faith by trusting Him again and again. We are supposed to learn from the lessons He is teaching us so we can grow in faith. God became so angry with the Israelites that He sentenced them to forty years, a year for each day that they searched the land, in the wilderness. The spies (except for Joshua and Caleb) who searched the land and "brought up an evil report," causing the people to complain "died by the plague before the LORD" (Num. 14:37). They suffered death for their disobedience and unbelief. The remaining congregation, those twenty years and older who complained, had to wander in the wilderness until all who disbelieved died. They never saw the Promised Land.

Their suffering was spiritual, physical, and emotional wandering—not going backward and not going forward, just staying in a dry desert, an uninhabitable land, for life. All they had to look forward to for the next forty years was death. Just think how miserable it would be to have no direction from God, just to wander around aimlessly with no purpose in life because of disobedience, never receiving the blessings God had promised.

This would be like running on our racetracks, and suddenly we come upon hurdles. We don't want to jump over them, so we turn around and try to run back to where we came from, but we can't because the tracks are no longer there. So we just stand there and never go any further in the race.

It certainly was not God's intention for them to wander in the wilderness. When they left Egypt God's plan was to take them through the wilderness and prepare them for the Promised Land. As they were going through the wilderness God was trying to teach them to depend on Him and trust in Him, to have patience and longsuffering, and gain strength through the different trials or tests He took them through. But they did not want to go through any trials. They decided they would rather go back to Egypt than experience any more tests.

Sometimes we would rather go back to doing the things we used to do because it's easier. It's harder to do something we have never done before. Many Christians just give up and go back into the world.

The Israelites were used to giving their flesh what it wanted, when it wanted it, and how it wanted it. They did not want what God wanted, when God wanted it, and how God wanted it, so they rebelled against God through disobedience because of unbelief.

Many times we do not want what God wants for us. His plan for our lives may not seem as wonderful as we expected it to be. We may think God's plan does not make sense or that His timing is wrong. Maybe we think our way of doing things is better than God's way of doing things. We may ask these questions: "How does God know what is best for us?" or "How can this be God's plan when we don't like what He wants us to do?" or "Don't we have the right to plan our own lives?"

These are all signs of unbelief in God's divine plan and His sovereign will for our lives. We may think these things, but if we begin to take it further and rebel against God's plan for us by going in an opposite direction or doing whatever our old nature wants to do, we become disobedient, just like the Israelites.

When the Israelites realized what they had done and how they sinned against God, they decided to go up to the top of the mountain to the Promised Land. Accepting God's blessings, which they rejected before and which God took away. But Moses informed them that they would be disobeying God if they went there, that they would not prosper, and that God would not protect them from their enemies because they turned away from Him.

Even in acknowledging their sin, they did not realize the consequence, which was that they would never under any circumstances go into the Promised Land. God's decision was final; He'd had enough of their disobedience. But they decided to go up there anyway; their enemies beat them and drove them back so they could not enter the Promised Land (Num. 14:39–45).

This is the same thing that could happen in our Christian lives. Once God has had enough of our consistent disobedience and He pronounces His chastisements upon us, there is nothing we can do to change God's mind. It will be too late then to acknowledge and agree with God that we have sinned so that He will withdraw the chastisement or give us the blessings that were promised.

While we are running on our racetracks and we encounter hurdles, some of us begin to think to ourselves (so no one can hear us, of course), "I am not going through this…this being a Christian stuff is too hard…I had fewer problems when I was in the world" or "It doesn't take all that…I have been serving God for years—why do I have to go through this now?" or " I'll do something else for God to make Him happy so that He can bless me…God wants me to be happy" or "It's too hard—this can't be of God…God wants me to do *what*?…Forget this new life in Christ stuff—I am going back into the (old) world."

These thoughts cause some Christians to get out of the Christian Olympics. God allowed a hurdle to be put in front of them, and they refused to jump over it. They tried to run around it, but it was still there blocking their way. So they turned around. But they could not run backward, over their old tracks, because the tracks are like a conveyer belt that is constantly in a forward motion. They have to get off of the tracks, get out of the race, and go back into the world—or they just stand in front of the hurdles never finishing the race.

Staying in the race without jumping over the hurdles is like running on a treadmill; your feet are moving but you are not going anywhere, just like the Israelites. There are exercises athletes do that involve running in place—that is, moving your feet and legs as if you are marching while standing still, not going anywhere.

There are many Christians who go to church, do church work, and are involved in ministry but have not jumped over the hurdles God has allowed to be put before them. Therefore, they are running in place because those hurdles are keeping them from going any further. The hurdles will help them to grow spiritually and to become stronger, but that will not happen if they just stand there running in place. In the Christian life we either progress to a deeper, stronger walk with God, becoming a mature Christian or we just stay the same way we were when we first became Christians, as a baby (1 Pet. 2:2).

If we don't jump over the hurdles that are there to prepare us for God's blessings, but continue to be disobedient not believing that God knows what is best for us, then when He has had enough His chastisements will be final and the blessings will be withdrawn forever. Just as with the Israelites, we can't have the promised blessings without undergoing the preparations for them.

In the Old Testament book of Jonah, the prophet tells how he was chastised because of his disobedience to God. God had a mission he wanted Jonah to do, which was to go to the great city Nineveh, the capital of the Assyrian Empire, and to cry out against it because of their wickedness. Instead of obeying God, Jonah took off and tried to run away from God to Tarshish on a ship (Jonah 1:1–3). He did not want to do what God told him to do. Many who are in the ministry have the same problem of not wanting to go where God wants them to go in order to preach.

Jonah did not realize that it is impossible to flee from the presence of God. Somehow all of us think at times that we can do or say something and God will not know about it. We may think, "It's too early in the morning" or "It's dark outside; God won't see us." But the darkness and the light are alike to Him. Or we may think things and don't think that

God heard our thoughts. But He understands the thoughts that are so deep in our mind, even before they have been formulated into thoughts. We forget about one of God's attributes, and that is His omnipresence.

I don't know whether Jonah ever read what King David wrote in Psalm 139, but if he did he would have known that even if he would "dwell in the uttermost parts of the sea" (verse 9), God would be there also. We may not want God to find us when we try to run away from Him. On the other hand, when we really need Him we may feel that we cannot find Him. But because of the omnipresence of God, He is everywhere present at the same time. He will always be right there for us when we want Him there—and also when we don't.

God let Jonah know that he could try to run but he could not hide, by sending a mighty whirlwind that tossed the ship about and threatened to shatter it. The mariners became afraid, called on their gods, and began to cast their wares into the sea to lighten the ship. Jonah did not know what was going on because he had gone down into the ship to lie down and was in a deep sleep. Jonah was so content that he was able to fall asleep; he thought that by leaving the city where God spoke to him he would not hear any more from God. He thought God was only in that city, so if he left and went to Tarshish, surely God's presence would not be there.

But before the ship could arrive in Tarshish, the shipmaster came to Jonah and woke him up out of his deep sleep. He probably could not understand how Jonah could be sleeping at a time like that. He told Jonah to get up and call upon his God (they called on their gods and nothing happened) to see if He could keep them from perishing. All who were on the ship called on their gods and lightened the ship by throwing their wares into the sea, but that did not stop the wind from tossing the ship.

Since they had done everything they could do, they

began to realize that all of this was happening for a reason and that someone must be the cause of it. So they decided to cast lots, and the lot fell upon Jonah. Then they questioned Jonah and wanted to know why this evil was happening to them. They wanted to know everything there was to know about Jonah. What was his occupation? Where did he come from? What was his country? Of what people was he? Jonah told them that he was a Hebrew and feared the God of heaven who made the sea and the dry land. God used His creation to get the attention of Jonah. Jonah told them he fled from the presence of the Lord, and then they knew that it was because of Jonah that this evil had come upon them. The men questioned Jonah as to why he did it and began to be terribly afraid.

Sometimes the world has to suffer along with us. If unbelievers are near us when God chastises us they will get the punishment too. Jonah's disobedience not only put his life in jeopardy but also the lives of the mariners. Then the men asked Jonah what should they do with him to calm the sea. Jonah had to admit that it was because of his disobedience that the whirlwind was tossing the ship. Jonah knew why he and the mariners were suffering. He did not have to think a long time, ask someone, or pray about it. If we are honest with ourselves we know whether our suffering is from disobedience to God, a test of our faith, or persecution for being a Christian.

When we suffer, the first thing we must do is ask why we are suffering. Is it chastisement, a test, or persecution? Once we discover the reason, then we can continue to run in the race accordingly. We cannot ignore our suffering, pretend that it does not exist, or "rebuke it in the name of Jesus," because it will not go away. It is part of being in the Christian race or competition.

If it is chastisement, then we must do whatever it is God wants us to do or confess our sins and stop doing whatever it was we were doing that was wrong. If not, there will be more and more chastisement until we are obedient to God. If it is a test, we have to finish the test and pass it in order to increase our faith and receive our blessings from God. If we don't finish and pass our test we won't be at the spiritual level God wants us to be in order to receive His blessings. We will lose our blessings just like the Israelites who wandered in the wilderness.

If it's because of persecution, we have to endure it for as long as God allows it. The Bible says that we who live in a godly way will suffer persecution (2 Tim. 3:12). If we try to stop the persecution, then we will be living like the world. Later in this chapter we will discuss how to endure persecution.

After Jonah confessed that the mariners' lives were in danger because of him, he offered a solution to the mariners that would quiet the sea. That was to cast him into the sea. Jonah did not want the mariners to be in any more danger because of him, so this was a way for him to receive his punishment alone. God used His creation to go after Jonah. The mariners tried to row the ship to land, but the sea was tossing the ship against it. They were trying their best to do something other than to throw Jonah into the sea. Jonah was willing to face death for his disobedience, but the mariners were afraid to cast him into the sea. So they prayed to Jonah's God that He would not hold them responsible for Jonah's life, and they cast him into the sea.

As soon as Jonah was cast into the sea, the raging ceased. God wanted Jonah, and nothing but Jonah could be cast into the sea to make it calm. After they cast him into the sea the mariners began to fear Jonah's God, after seeing how He controlled the sea and could find them no matter where they were. So they offered sacrifices to God and made vows. Jonah did not die. God the Creator, who sent the whirlwind to toss the ship, appointed another one of His creatures, a great fish, to swallow up Jonah. All of God's creations recognize their Creator and obey Him, responding to His every command.

As human beings we are the only creatures who were made with a will of our own. God will not make us do anything; He wants us to obey Him out of our own free will. He just wants us to recognize, like the rest of His creation, that He is our creator, that He is sovereign, and that He does what He wants to do, when He wants to do it, and how He wants to do it. In turn God wants us to have faith and trust that He knows what is best for us because He loves us. Because of His love for us and our love for Him, we obey willingly.

God performed another miracle with His creation by preparing one of His great fish to swallow Jonah and leaving him in his belly for three days and three nights. While Jonah was in the fish's belly he prayed to God and thanked Him for saving his life. Then God caused the fish to vomit Jonah onto the dry land. The Lord told Jonah to rise up and for the second time told him to go and preach to the great city of Nineveh the message He had given him before. This time Jonah obeyed God and went into the city of Nineveh and preached, and the people believed God and turned from their evil ways.

I imagine some of you are saying, "I guess after all that, he would obey God! I would have too!" But remember the Israelites; after all of the miracles He performed in their lives, they were still disobedient.

This is like running on our racetracks and suddenly there is something God wants us to do (or somewhere He wants us to go) in ministry that we just don't want to do. There could be many reasons why we don't want to obey God. Jonah admits his reason in Jonah 4:2: he wanted God to punish the people of Nineveh, but God would not do that because they turned from their evil ways. He ran away because he did not want to preach to them to give them an opportunity to repent. He did not want them to have a forty-day warning. He may have felt the way we might feel sometimes when people do evil things; we don't want to give them any mercy or warn them. We want to watch God sentence or punish them and offer no second chances.

Another reason may be because no other prophets preached to any nationality other than to the Hebrews. The people of Nineveh were the ungodly and were non-Hebrew. Perhaps Jonah felt God should destroy them because of these reasons. We have to be careful that we don't limit our ministry to certain people or nationalities. We also have to have mercy on the ungodly and accept them when God forgives them and they become Christians. We should not be like Jonah and resist witnessing to people so they won't repent and God can send them to hell. The mission God wants us to accomplish in ministry will remain. Just like with Jonah, God will ask us again and again to obey Him, and our mission will stay in front of us until we become obedient to God and accomplish it.

Part 2
The Workout

Suffering for Righteousness: More Precious Than Gold
Even the athletes who follow all the rules their coaches and trainers impose experience suffering, because that is part of being an athlete. This type of suffering is welcomed as well as expected; if they didn't have some aches and pains they would not be working out or exercising enough in order to compete at their maximum potential.

So it is in the Christian Olympics; suffering for righteousness is part of being in the competition. The first type of righteous suffering is trials or the test of our faith.

The biblical book of 1 Peter, which was written for

suffering Christians, says this in chapter 1, verse 7: "that the trial of your faith, being much more precious than of gold that perisheth, though it be tried with fire, might be found unto praise and honor and glory at the appearing of Jesus Christ:". This verse gives us insight into the high value God places on our numerous and various trials. When our faith is tested, no matter how severe, it is more precious than gold, which is perishable. It will result in the praise, glory, and honor when Jesus Christ appears.

Not all suffering is chastisement, a result of disobedience, as in the case of the Israelites and Jonah. It can be a test as it was with a man name Job, to whom an entire book of the Bible's Old Testament records is devoted and which is named after him. The first chapter of Job begins by telling us that Job lived in the land of Uz, and he was perfect, upright, and feared God. Not only did he fear God, but he also turned away from evil. Job was blessed with a large family, seven sons and three daughters. He had many possessions, had a great household, and "was the greatest of all the men of the east" (verse 3). Job was so righteous that he would offer a burnt offering for his family just in case they had sinned or cursed God in their hearts. Since there was no man on earth like Job, there was a conversation about him between the Lord and Satan, which was discussed briefly in chapter two.

It is remarkable to have an opportunity to listen in on a conversation the Lord had with our competitor, Satan. It was recorded in Job 1:6–12 through 2:1–7. Job, of course, was unaware of this conversation. Let's listen in on the entire conversation.

Satan, who was called Lucifer (Is. 14:12–17), was the leader of the angels in heaven. When he sinned he was put out of heaven along with the angels who followed him (Luke 10:18). These fallen angels are called demons, and Satan is their leader. Satan and his demons now rule the world and have authority over the atmospheric heaven above the earth (John 12:31, Eph. 2:2). Although he was put out of heaven, he still tries to mingle with the good or unfallen angels when they present themselves before the Lord.

One day Satan came along with the sons of God (angels) who came to present themselves before the Lord. God asked Satan where he had come from. Satan said he had come from going back and forth and walking up and down in the earth. Can you just picture Satan walking on the earth swinging his arms as if he has nothing better to do, looking for trouble, trying to find something he can accuse Christians of as they are running on their racetracks? He keeps going back and forth and back and forth, up and down and up and down on the earth. The Lord knew what Satan was looking for, so He began a conversation with him about a man who cannot be compared to anyone on the earth—His servant Job, who was perfect and feared God.

Then Satan's reply was that Job didn't fear God without reason. In other words, he is saying that Job has a reason for fearing God. There are some things Satan cannot see, and among those things are our hearts and our motives. He may think he knows why we do things or why we fear God, but he cannot see deep down in the recesses of our hearts the way God can.

Then Satan explained why he believed Job feared God and why he was upright and perfect and turned away from evil. He told the Lord it was because He had put a fence around him, his house, and all he had. What he is saying is that the Lord put His protection all around Job and everything he possessed, which meant no evil or harm could touch Job. Have you ever felt or seen the protection of the Lord around you? Have you ever seen something happen to someone else, but it did not happen to you and you were standing right there? Or your neighbors' houses were destroyed but yours was still standing? This is what Satan meant. He went on further to say that not only was Job protected but God had also blessed the work of his hands. Satan was saying that whatever Job did, the Lord blessed it and caused his possessions to increase in the land. Everything Job touched was blessed by the Lord.

So Satan thought those were the reasons why Job feared God. He told God that if He touched all that Job had, Job would curse Him to His face. What he was asking the Lord to do was to remove the protective fence around Job so he could be touched. Satan felt that Job had everything, including an easy life with no problems. In other words, who wouldn't serve God when everything is going well? Once Job had experienced tragedy, he wouldn't serve God anymore and would blame God for it.

So the Lord gave Satan permission to touch everything that Job had, but not to touch him. Have you ever experienced a time in your life when you felt or could see that God removed His fence of protection around you? You were hurt along with everyone else. Your house was destroyed along with everyone else's. Now the Lord allows Job to be tested to show Satan that Job will serve Him even in the midst of tragedies.

While we are running on our racetracks and God allows hurdles to test our faith in Him, will we jump over them? Can we pass tests like these? Would we serve God if He allowed tragedies to occur in our lives, especially if we are walking uprightly? Sometimes we can understand it if we go through adversities because of our disobedience, but it may be very difficult to accept if we have been living righteously before God as Job was.

Let's see what Satan did with Job's possessions and how Job handled it. One day while Job's sons and daughters were eating and drinking wine in their oldest brother's house, a messenger came to Job and told him the Sabeans (the descendants of Sheba) had come and taken his oxen and asses, and had slain his servants with the edge of the sword. While this messenger was speaking a second person came and told Job the fire of God had come down from heaven and burned and consumed his sheep and the servants. While that person was speaking, a third person came and told Job that the Chaldeans had come and taken camels away and slain the servants with the edge of the sword. While he was speaking a fourth person came to Job to tell him that while his sons and daughters were feasting a great wind came from over the wilderness and it smote the four corners of the house, which fell on them and killed them.

We can see the power Satan has to steal, to kill, and to destroy (John 10:10), which in this case God permitted. Within a matter of minutes Job lost everything he had. It was not a gradual loss that expanded over the years or a sum of calamities that occurred during a lifetime. It happened all at once.

This is similar to what can happen to us while we are running on our racetracks, and suddenly a hurdle appears. Before we complete our jump over that hurdle, another one appears. After we have completed jumping over the first hurdle and are trying to jump over the second hurdle, suddenly the third hurdle appears. And finally, as we are completing the jump over the third hurdle, the fourth one appears. This is what is called hurdling back-to-back. Losing a home, job, personal possessions, and everything you own, as well as your family—all these losses are hurdles. These hurdles are not a punishment when you know you are living righteously; they are a test to see if you will be faithful to God.

We know this now, only because of this and other examples in the Scriptures. But remember, Job did not know it was a test; he did not know about the conversation about him that the Lord had with Satan. Most likely he had never seen or heard of anyone who was righteous, or maybe even unrighteous, losing everything in a matter of minutes.

Have you ever had something happen to you that you had never seen or heard of happening to anyone else before?

Let's see how Job handled this: verses 20–22 indicate that Job did not get angry with the Lord or sin, but he fell down on the ground and worshiped Him. He was also thankful and blessed the Lord, because he realized that everything he had the Lord had given to him. He came into this world with nothing, and he will leave with nothing. What he was saying was that the same Lord who gives is the same Lord who takes away. He's not going to bless the Lord when He gives him things and fail to bless Him when He takes those things away, because He is still the same Lord. This is how God wants us to handle hurdling back-to-back. No matter how fast or how many hurdles appear before us as we are attempting to complete our jump, we must continue jumping to pass the test while we bless and thank God.

Physical Suffering

So Job passed his test, proving that he was not serving God just because of His protection around him and the possessions He had blessed him with. He was perfect and upright, feared God, and turned from evil because he loved God.

But that was not good enough for Satan; he still thought Job had not suffered enough. He probably thought Job must not have placed much value on his possessions if he could give them up so easily. Satan thought there must be something else that could hurt Job more to cause him to fail the test, so he mingled again with the sons of God when they came to present themselves before the Lord. The Lord asked him again where he had come from, and he gave the same answer. The Lord asked him again about His servant Job. From these passages we get a clear picture of the role of one of our spectators and competitors, Satan. He is always trying to get permission from God to put hurdles in front of us while we are running on our racetracks.

We have to keep in mind that these hurdles are only a test of our faith in God, which He allows and which is more precious than gold, though it be tried in the fire. But for Satan, they are designed to get us to walk away from God and not finish our race. The Lord continued His conversation with Satan, asking him again about His servant Job, saying that there was no one on earth like him. He was perfect and upright, feared God, and turned from evil. Then the Lord told Satan that Job was still holding fast to his integrity even though He allowed Satan to destroy his possessions without cause.

There are four very important lessons we learn from the conversations between God and Satan. First, it was God who suggested that Satan consider Job because he was upright. Secondly, in all he did to Job, destroying everything he owned, Job was still thankful and blessed God. Number three, Satan had to get God's permission to touch Job and his possessions. The final and fourth point is there was nothing Job did that caused the calamities to come upon him.

These four principle truths are what we must keep in mind when calamities strike us. We first have to find out if they are trials. If God has not shown us something we have done wrong, and we have no unconfessed sins in our lives, then it is a trial. Usually if calamities occur and we have been disobedient to God then we will know, as Jonah did, that it is chastisement. Knowing our calamities are not a result of our sins will help us to endure them. After we recognize them as a trial then we can accept the fact that God had suggested Satan consider us because of our righteous living.

Next, we have learned that Satan could not touch us or our possessions without God's permission. After accepting these principle truths we can bless God as Job did. At the time, the only thing Job knew was that he was upright and continued to fear God. He did not know God had talked with Satan about his righteousness. He did not know God allowed Satan to touch him and that the righteous do indeed suffer. Even though he did not know what we now know, he still blessed God. A lesson we can take from Job, even if we don't understand our calamity, is to continue to bless God.

Now that we know these four points we can jump over our hurdles of trials. Knowing that God has allowed them as testing and not as punishment, we can bless and thank God for them, because they are intended for His praise and glory.

Then Satan probably remembered their conversation from before, when the Lord gave him permission to touch Job's possessions but not to touch him. He says to the Lord in Job 2:5 that if He touches his bones and his flesh, he will curse Him to His face. The very thing God had told Satan not to touch in their earlier conversation is exactly what he seeks the Lord's permission to touch now.

Our competitor, Satan, remembers every word God says. He never forgets them and will remind God when it is convenient for him to do so. The Lord answered Satan and gave him permission to touch Job's bones and his flesh but not to take his life. Then Satan left the presence of the Lord and caused Job to break out in boils and sores (the Hebrew meaning being burning and inflammation) from the bottom of his feet to the top of his head. Job then took a potsherd to scrape himself and sat down in the middle of the ashes. A potsherd consists of a piece of an earthen vessel; he used it to relieve the intolerable itching caused by the boils and to remove the boils.

Now Job's bones were in terrible pain because of these boils all over him, causing his body to burn and become sore. Job was sick, but he did not know why; again he had not heard the conversation the Lord had with Satan. But because of what happened to Job, it is a revelation to us that God can test us by allowing Satan to make us sick, in order to test our faith in God through our pain. While we are running on our racetracks, hurdles of sickness can appear before us, and we have to jump over them in order to finish the race. Even those who are not in the race get sick and have calamities. But when it happens because we are in the race, it is only a test of trials.

After Job got sick and remembered the other calamities that had befallen him, his wife, who was not mentioned earlier, asked him if he was going to retain his integrity or if he was going to curse God and die. We spoke about another competitor in chapter 2, called the flesh, our old nature, which is competing against us. But the old nature from someone else can compete against us also.

This is how the competitor, the flesh, can work through the old natures of spouses and family members to get us to give up our faith in God. This is what Job's wife was trying to do. As we are running on our racetracks we may have family members who may or may not be in the race or have gotten out of the race. They may see us running by and say things through their old nature to try to stop us from running.

According to Matthew 10:36, our enemies can be those of our own households. We must recognize that it is our competitor, the flesh, that is speaking, but we have to keep on running towards the finish line, running and fighting the old nature with our two-edged sword. Job answered his wife by saying she was speaking the way foolish women speak and asked her if it was right that they should receive good from the Lord and not bad. Job was saying the same thing he said before, that the Lord gives and the Lord takes away. Job passed his test, even after he became sick with so much pain. He did not sin with his lips.

You can imagine that people all throughout the land had heard about the evil that happened to Job. When his three friends, Eliphaz the Temanite, Bildad the Shuhite, and Zophar the Naamathite, heard of it, they made an appointment to meet together at Job's house to mourn with him and to comfort him. As they were approaching Job from a distance they did not recognize him. Apparently the boils that were all over his body had disfigured him to the point that he was unrecognizable. When they saw that it was Job, they began to weep with their voices and cut out their upper robes, sprinkling dust on their heads. They sat down on the ground with him for seven days and nights. They did not say anything to him because they could see he was in great pain.

But on the eighth day, Job began to speak. He cursed his life and wished he had died after he had been born (Job 3:1–26). Have you ever been so sick and in so much pain that you wished you could die? The very thing you feared the most had happened to you, causing you to wish you had died on the day you were born. We do not know how long Job suffered so severely, but it was for a long time. Our trials can last minutes, hours, days, months, years, or even a lifetime.

The first person to speak after Job spoke was his friend Eliphaz (Job chapters 4 and 5). First he asked Job if they could have a word with him or would that cause him to become weary. When people are very sick and in a lot of pain their visitors can make them tired. But he followed up with the question, "Who can restrain themselves from speaking?" and then he began to speak. He began by acknowledging how Job had comforted those who were in trouble, but now Job was in trouble and it had made him weary.

It seems as though Eliphaz would comfort Job, since he knew Job had comforted others. Maybe Eliphaz was just trying to be a little sarcastic, the way someone would say, "You helped everyone else; why can't you help yourself?" Or maybe he was teasing him as if he was a crybaby: "You act like you can't take it, now that it's your turn." So Eliphaz asked Job if it was true that the fear of God was his confidence and the uprightness of his ways was his hope—as if to ask why that wasn't enough to comfort him. This was all Job had to hold on to, but he was still in physical pain. The pain was affecting him emotionally and spiritually, because he was not able to understand why he was suffering.

The only thing Eliphaz and the rest of his company of friends could say to Job over and over again, in many different ways, was that only the unrighteous suffer. He continued to tell Job that he couldn't possibly be innocent and that he needed to seek God. He said that men reap what they sow and that God was chastising him. Then he told him about a dream he had. Job said that the burden of his grief and calamity was so heavy that he had spoken hastily. He felt that God was against him, and he wished that God would grant his request to die.

Emotional and Psychological Suffering

Here we see the emotional suffering Job was trying to endure. His only hope was for his life to end. He did not see any other way to escape the deep physical pain he was experiencing. Physical suffering often affects our emotions. We think and say things that under normal circumstances we ordinarily would not say. At that particular time, though, that is the way we feel. Job's friend however, did not help the situation with his comments. Job had to rebuke his friend Eliphaz, telling him he should show kindness to someone who is afflicted (6:14).

Before he spoke, his friend acknowledged that Job was in physical pain and could hear his emotional pain through the words he said. But he made things worse by trying to get Job to doubt his innocence. What he needed was comforting words, which could not heal the physical pain but could heal his emotional pain. Job went on to tell Eliphaz that the comfort he had was his bed, but now he has scared him with the dreams he told him about and had terrified him with his visions (7:13–14).

Then Job's friend Bildad began to speak and told Job that if he was an upright man, by now God would have raised him up. God will not reject a perfect man. Bildad did not believe Job was righteous; his reasoning was that God does not allow someone to go through what Job was going through if the person is righteous.

Have you ever gone through a trial and your Christian friends looked at you funny and told you it must be your fault? That if you were a true Christian this trial never would have happened? They say: "God doesn't do things like that" or "God would not allow something like that to happen to you." At a time when you needed comfort, their words just added to your calamities and grief.

Job's friend Zophar then spoke and told Job that if he would turn away from his sin, things would get better (11:13–20). He made Job feel inferior to him as though Job did not know anything about God, which was what Job said when he responded to Zophar. Job called his friends forgers of lies and physicians of no value (13:4). Their so-called healing meant nothing when they were stitching wounds with lies. How could they heal with lies? You can't repair something by sewing it with lies, Job told them.

But through everything Job proclaimed: "Though he slay me, yet will I trust in him :..." (13:15). Even if God kills him, or he dies from his illness, he will wait with hope. The word "trust" in this verse is the Hebrew word *yachal*, which means "to...wait with hope." That same Hebrew word is used for the word "wait" when Job says "...I will wait, till my change come." (14:14). Waiting goes together with hope, because it is difficult to wait without hope.

When we are going through our test of trials we have to do our spiritual exercises: walking in the spirit, walking by faith, and stretching by faith as we wait with hope.

The Christian Olympics

We see in chapter 15 that Eliphaz speaks again and asks Job what he knows that they don't know. They are gray-headed and aged men, older than his father. They are telling Job that because they are older than he is they have more wisdom than he has. They are right, and he is wrong.

In chapter 16, Job responds by saying to them that they are miserable comforters. Now we can hear the cry in Job's voice, when he asks if they think he would speak to them the way they have spoken to him if they were in his place. Would he shake his head at them? Can you imagine them shaking their heads at Job in judgment as if it is Job's own fault that he is suffering? That he brought all of this on himself? He would say things that would strengthen them and ease their pain. But his company has just been misery.

Job's visitors made matters worse for Job, as if he was not suffering enough. In chapter 18, Bildad speaks again and tells Job that what he is going through is an example of what happens to those who don't know God. In chapter 19, Job has had enough and asks his friends, "How long will ye vex my soul, and break me in pieces with words?" (verse 2). He points out that they have blamed him ten times.

Then he pleads with them that if he did something wrong, it was something he did to himself. In other words, why would it concern them if he did something wrong to himself and is suffering for it? It is not as if he did something to them or to someone else. He then tries to get them to understand what he was beginning to see, that it was God who had caused his afflictions. Job's friends kept pointing out (probably with their fingers pointing at him as they were shaking their heads) that suffering is for the ungodly and not the righteous.

But Job continued to tell them he is righteous and God was allowing these afflictions to come upon him. In other words Job is trying to make them see (though he has never seen anything like this happen before) that the righteous must suffer, because he is suffering. Job goes on to explain his tremendous emotional pain (verses 13–20) and that God has put his "brethren far from him," his "kinfolk have failed," and his "familiar friends have forgotten" him. He calls his servants, and they don't answer him. He says his "breath is strange" to his wife; those who live in his house and his maids "count [him] as a stranger." Young children reject him, his friends have rejected him, and those whom he loved have turned against him.

Not only was he an alien to his friends and family but also his bones have cleaved to his skin and flesh. Job then pleads with his visitors over and over again to have pity on him because the hand of God has touched him. Job asked them why they continued to pursue him as God did. But through all of this Job believed that his Redeemer lives and that after worms destroy his body when he dies, he will see God with his own eyes (19:25).

Can you see the fight Job was having with his friends? Not only will spectacles suffer, but while they are suffering they have to continue to fight. The fight can be with our old nature and with the old nature of our families, friends, and other spectacles. This is why we have to practice discipline and do our spiritual exercises, so no matter how weak we are physically, we will be spiritually strong enough to continue to run in the race and fight our competitors. Just because we may become weak physically does not mean our competitors are going to stop competing with us. Remember, the Christian race is not physical anyway; it is spiritual. But if we are not careful, our physical condition can affect us spiritually.

Chapter 20 records Zophar's final punch, about the ways of the wicked. Job fights back in chapter 21, stating that the prosperous and the bad die all the same and that their comforts are vain and their answers are false. Chapter 22 records Eliphaz's final punch in which he tells Job to return to the Almighty. In Chapters 23–24, Job fights back with another punch. He tries to tell them that he would find God if only he could; can't they see he is talking to God, but God does not hear him? Have you ever had to try to explain to other Christians that you are praying? You are not in the predicament you are in because you are not praying. He had the assurance that when his testing was finished, he would come forth as gold because he had kept God's way (23:10–11).

Now it is Bildad's turn for his final punch in Chapter 25, asking Job the question, "How can a man be righteous before God?" Job fights back with his answers in Chapters 26–28. He makes a profound statement at the end of chapter 28, in verse 28. He said, "...Behold, the fear of the Lord, that is wisdom; and to depart from evil is understanding." Even though Job was suffering physically and emotionally he was being strengthened spiritually, which gave him the strength to defend himself from his friends' punches ("...though our outward man perish, yet the inward man is renewed day by day." 2Cor.4:16). Because he feared the Lord, the Lord revealed to him what wisdom was and also that departing from evil, as he had done, was understanding. We will all suffer, but only the sufferings of the righteous work toward their own benefit. It is for their good and for divine purposes (Rom. 8:28).

Job began to give us a clear picture, in chapter 29, about how things were for him in the past—the way he lived before his calamities, when he lost everything. He began to reminisce about how things were before he became sick.

Have you ever had a calamity, an affliction, or an illness, and you thought about the way things used to be? Job had his own established place in the street of the city where he would sit down and speak (verses 7–10). People of the city listened to him and respected him. He sat as head and dwelt as a king, a counselor in the troop (army), "as one who comforteth the mourners" (verse 25). Are you the one who comforts those who mourn? Do people hang on your every word when you speak? He was respected and honored, and the people of the community listened to his words.

But now he is experiencing humiliation, which is causing him to suffer psychologically. Job said that those younger than he, the children of fools, men without names, are singing and laughing at him. They had hatred and disgust for him, they stayed far away from him, and they spat in his face (30:9–10). They would tease him and, as we would say, "pick on him." They even made up a song to taunt him with. You can imagine what they were singing. Something like, "He used to have everything, but now he don't have nothing!" Can you think of some songs you may have been taunted with?

Isn't it strange that those who would taunt and tease the righteous when they are suffering, like Job, are those who are poor and foolish? Those who need help themselves but cannot see that they are in a similar or worse predicament? The people who were taunting him were hungry and ate broom-tree roots for food. They were desolate and were driven away from everyone else and lived in caves. Job was pointing out the nerve that people like that had to have to tease him (30:1–8).

Because he used to be rich and now has lost everything, they want to tease him and be mean to him. In the same way, it is also strange that when someone is down and out, sick, homeless, or wandering in the streets people take advantage of them. As if things can't get any worse, sometimes human nature likes to see the person suffer more. They add to it or just think that what they do to them won't hurt or doesn't matter because they have already reached rock bottom.

They are treated like a pile of trash that someone just

dumped where it should not be. Have you ever noticed how a small pile of trash gets bigger and bigger until someone cleans it up? The reason for this is that because the trash is already there, people think it is not going to hurt anything if they just add a little bit to the pile. "Why not? Everyone else is putting their trash there," they figure.

If suddenly everything God had given to us was taken away, there would be people who might say, "Hah!" "Hah!" We would be the laughingstock of the neighborhood. Job was feeling as if he was fair prey. Since God had allowed him to be afflicted, the people felt they could do anything they wanted to him (30:11–15).Have you ever had people take advantage of your bad circumstances?

Now Job describes in detail the way he was suffering physically (30:16–24). He felt that when he called out to God, He did not hear him. His days of affliction had taken hold of him, his bones pierced him in the night, and there was no rest to his gnawing. The power of his disease had changed his clothing. The same clothing he wore before he was sick now looked like a disguise on him.

Sometimes a person can be so sick that their clothing doesn't fit them the same way anymore, and they look unrecognizable. They look like a different person even though they have on their same clothing. Have you ever seen someone sick and could not recognize them, and someone else had to tell you who they were?

He continues to describe his suffering (30:27–31). His heart bubbles up and cannot keep still. He felt like a brother to the jackals and a friend to the ostriches. His sickness was so bad that he no longer felt like a human being. Perhaps his mourning, pain, and grief could relate more to their howling, their long, loud, wailing cries. They could tell the story of how he felt and sing his song better than he or other human beings could. His skin was black, and his bones were burned by the heat.

The Christian Olympics

In Chapter 31, Job continues to prove his innocence by listing an account of all of his good deeds. He stated he had never been unfaithful to his wife even in his heart. How many men can say that? If he had mistreated his servants, the poor, the widows, or the fatherless, or rejoiced in his wealth and not given God the glory, then he should be punished.

Job continues by adding another good deed: if he had not entertained strangers, then he should be punished, but he was not guilty of that or any of the other things. He did not even rejoice in the destruction of those who hated him. How many of us would not rejoice over the destruction of our enemies and those who hate us? Some of us are waiting and looking forward to the day when God will punish our enemies. We want God to "get them" the way a lion devours his prey.

Job never let his riches go to his head or trusted in his riches. He always looked out for the unfortunate and acknowledged God as his Creator.

He was a God-fearing person, and if he had done something wrong, then he felt he should be punished for it. How many of us could handle being as wealthy as Job was? Even though he was wealthy, he still feared God and worshiped Him. He taught his family to do the same. He was still kind to his servants and had compassion on the poor and needy. From his experiences, we saw he was the same person with his riches as he was when they were taken away. Would we be the same God-fearing people if we became wealthy? Would we act the same, talk the same, and treat people the same way?

But he continues to argue that he has done nothing wrong; if only his good deeds and his steps had been recorded! He did not know then what we know now, that all of our deeds are recorded in God's book.

Some people would take Job as being braggadocious or self-righteous, as his friends did. But they did accuse him of not being righteous, didn't they? Didn't he have to defend himself? He couldn't help it if he lived a righteous life; isn't that the reason God asked Satan to consider His servant Job in the first place? Wasn't he just being obedient to God? Didn't God say, "…ye shall be holy; for I am holy" (Lev. 11:44) and "Be ye therefore perfect, even as your Father which is in heaven is perfect." (Matt. 5:48)? Job concludes that he is innocent and suffering at the hand of God. His friends conclude that Job is not innocent and is therefore being punished for his sins. They could not answer any of Job's questions.

In Chapters 32–37, there are accounts of a fourth person, a young man who came to speak to Job. From his account, we can tell he was there all along listening to Job's three friends. He was never mentioned until this point. He waited until last to give his advice because the other three were older than he was. His name was Elihu, the son of Barachel the Buzite.

Elihu was angry with what he heard from Job and his three friends and held his comments as long as he could, giving respect to the elderly. He told Job that in this particular matter, he was not righteous, and if he could understand that, then God would forgive him and raise him up. He goes on to say that God repays man according to his works and does not do wicked things. Which is true—God will reward us according to our works, but He has not said we would never have trials too. It is also true that God does not do wicked things, but He does allow wicked things to happen.

Since Job refused to say he had sinned, Elihu's claim was that he was adding rebellion to his sin. Elihu felt he was perfect in knowledge, and Job did not have any knowledge. He insisted that when the righteous are afflicted, God shows them they had sinned. When they turn from their sin, they will prosper; if not they will perish. Elihu believed that Job was suffering due to his own wickedness and that Job could not change his mind about it.

The Christian Olympics

Have you ever gotten into a debate with your brothers or sisters in Christ, about God or the Bible? No matter how much you talked and no matter how much they talked, the debate ended without you coming to an agreement. Sometimes that leads to arguments, and everyone leaves angry. Only God could say who was right and who was wrong, which is what God does at the end of the book of Job. He was listening to the arguments and watching the fight. He comes in at the end as the referee to announce the winner. Will it be Brother Eliphaz, Brother Bildad, Brother Zophar, Brother Job, or Brother Elihu?

While we are running on our racetracks we will experience various trials. Some may be extreme suffering, as it was with Job, suffering no one can understand or be able to explain. Spectacles take notice of other spectacles who seem to have had an excessive amount of hurdles to jump over, especially if the hurdles appear consecutively. To them it may seem excessive because they've never had that many hurdles to jump over before.

We must also keep in mind that some hurdles take a long time to jump over, unlike the Olympic Games where it only takes a few seconds. Our jumps over hurdles could last minutes, hours, days, weeks, years, or a lifetime. They could be *l-o-n-g* jumps, which means we jumped, but we did not complete the jump over the hurdle; the jump is not completed until the trial is over. Picture this: you are running on your racetrack and suddenly a hurdle appears. You jump, but you stay in position hanging over the hurdle. You have to stay in that position until the test is over before you can complete the jump.

This is when other spectacles come by to comfort you and encourage you to hang up there until you can complete the jump. But like Job's friends, some spectacles cannot believe God would allow the righteous to suffer and not let them complete the jump, especially when they have started jumping over the hurdle many years ago and have not completed the jump yet. Like Job's friends, they think you must have committed a terrible sin. So instead of comforting you, they tell you that all you have to do is confess your sins and then you can complete the jump. The spectacle who is enduring his own trial tries to explain that he has not sinned; it is God who has not allowed him to complete his jump.

This is how it is for Christians who have been sick for many, many years and look like they are near death's door. They know they have been obedient to God and their sickness is not a chastisement from God. But visitors from their church insist that by now, they should have risen from their bed of affliction. "If only they would confess their sins, then God could raise them up," they would say, as they shake their heads and point their fingers. They would even start an argument with the afflicted about it and continue to hurt them with their words. They continue their assault on their emotions by trying to get them to doubt their faith in God.

How about those who come to counsel Christians who are going through trials of unemployment? No matter how hard they try to explain that they have looked everywhere but there is no work, their counselors insist they are not trying hard enough. Then they humiliate them by telling them there must be something wrong with them, because by now they should have a job. "There must be some sin in their life," they say, "because God would have made a way for them to find a job by now. What has it been now, ten years?" When the unemployed Christians explain that this is a trial they are going through and that God is teaching them to live by faith, their counselors who came to comfort them would just laugh.

How about pastors who could not find another church to pastor since their first assignment—say about twenty years ago? When they applied for a pastoral position at several churches, the search committees could not understand why they have not been pastors for twenty years. The pastors explain that for the past twenty years, they have been praying and seeking God to lead them to the church He wants them to shepherd, but God had not done so yet.

The search committee and others look at them strangely, shake their heads, and say, "There must be something wrong here. God does not do things like that. That's not of God. How can he have the gift and call to the pastorate and not be led by God to pastor other churches?" The pastors would say that this has been their test from God for twenty years, to which the committee would reply, "We are sorry. If this was God's doing, then you must not have been a good pastor twenty years ago, and God has been punishing you since then." "He must have been living in sin for twenty years, not praying and seeking God as he claims," some would also say. "That's why he could not find a church to pastor; no church wanted him."

What about Christians who have lost their entire families in fatal accidents or other tragedies? When friends and church members come to comfort them, they may say that their families must have sinned, so God was punishing them, as Job's friends said to him. Some would say, "I can see losing a few family members but not all of them. There must be something in their lives that God is not pleased with."

During our Christian race we will go through various trials, and many times there will be no one who can explain them nor understand them. But we have to know within ourselves that we are not being chastised for our sins. We are the only ones who can truly defend that in the sight of God, which is the only thing that will give us peace of mind during our trials. Knowing that we are not being chastised for something that we did or did not do relieves us of the heavy burdens of guilt and shame. Then we have to stand on the fact that we have walked with God as Job did and just wait with hope until the change comes.

While we are going through trials of testing, God begins to teach us about Himself. We learn things about God that we did not know before our trials. During our testing times, God will also show us things about ourselves. Whenever we see God in a deeper way or He reveals to us an aspect of His nature and attributes that we have never seen before, we see how minute we are and how majestic He is.

Job had been praying to God for an answer. He wanted to know why he was suffering and when it was going to end. Prayer is what helped Job to endure all of his calamities. Even though he did not know what was going on with him, he kept praying. He did not know why God was allowing this to happen to him, but he kept praying. Even when he felt that God was not answering his prayers, he continued to pray. When we are in similar circumstances only our breathing exercises, which is prayer, can help us endure. Prayer is what will help us to hang up there over our hurdles until our trial of testing is over and God allows us to complete the jump.

Finally in Chapters 38–41, God answers Job out of a whirlwind and addresses him with a series of questions in order to teach Job about his Creator. He began with a question, addressing Job as one who hides counsel with words without knowledge. Then He starts off by asking Job to make a vigorous effort, like a man, to answer His questions. The series of questions starts off with: Where was he when He laid the foundations of the earth? Who made the measurements? Who stretched the line upon it? Whereupon are the foundations fastened? Who laid the cornerstone? These were followed by many more questions God asked in order to show Job His many attributes—that He was the self-existing One and that He was the sovereign Creator of everything.

After God taught Job who He was, He asked Job if the one (speaking of Job) who argues with the Almighty, the self-sufficient, mighty One, should be the one to instruct

Him. God revealed to Job that during the time he was going through his trials, he was arguing with Him and instructing Him. This did not have anything to do with why he was suffering and what his friends accused him of. Remember what God told Satan, that Job was perfect. This was a private conversation that a servant, Job, had with his Lord about their personal relationship. God would address who won the argument and fight between Job and his friends later.

God had to teach him that He is God and that Job is just a man. Human beings cannot argue with the Creator or tell Him what to do. They can only be silent and listen to the instructions of the omniscient God.

God did not give Job the answers he wanted to hear. He wanted to know why he was suffering and how much longer it would last. But after God spoke, Job felt small compared to the almighty God. He felt ashamed that he questioned God. He was able to see less of himself and more of God. Job could not answer God; for the first time during his trials, he was at a loss for words. No longer was his suffering an issue for him. Then God went on to ask Job more questions that further explained His nature and attributes.

When God finished questioning him, Job acknowledged that God can do everything and knows everything, because He is the almighty God. Job admitted he had said things he did not understand, things that were too wonderful for him that he did not know. With this new knowledge and understanding about God, Job was able to see God more clearly. He heard about God with his ears and read about Him, but he did not see His omniscience as the Creator and the self-existing One. Our trials of testing help us gain a knowledge and understanding of God that we otherwise would not have known, which causes us to progress from just hearing God with our ears to seeing God with our eyes.

Now that Job could see God, he realized he was wrong to try to instruct and argue with the almighty God, which he did not realize before and which is why God had to teach him. God never holds us responsible for things we do not know. Job was so sorry about it that he despised himself and repented in dust and ashes. Job's actions truly revealed a righteous man. Even though he had not known what God just taught him, he repented for not knowing. He felt that even though he did not know, it was still a sin against the almighty God.

How many of us confess our unknown sins to God? He could have said to the Lord, "Why are you telling me this or showing me this now?" or "I didn't know it was wrong, so I'm not responsible for what I said." God still declared Job to be righteous, holy, and perfect, just as God has declared us righteous, holy, and perfect because of our faith in Jesus Christ. But that does not mean we don't sin. It just means we do all we know that God requires of us, and we confess our known sins continuously. It means our lives are in total submission to God's sovereign will, and when He reveals unknown sin to us, we don't rebel, but we are sorry and acknowledge it. Then we agree with God and turn away from sin the way Job did.

Not only does the flesh compete with spectacles through their own old natures or their families' old natures, but it also can compete through other spectacles' old natures, such as those of friends, acquaintances, and other Christians.

Job's friends are an example of how spectacles can allow their old nature to cause other spectacles to suffer. Spectacles are not in competition with one another, which we discussed extensively in previous chapters. But the old nature in every spectacle can be tempted to compete with other spectacles. We must not allow this to happen, and we can avoid it by doing what James 4:7 says: "Submit yourselves therefore to God. Resist the devil, and he will flee from you." Temptations can occur when spectacles cannot understand why other spectacles are suffering. They yield to the temptations by giving wrong advice and comfortless words, and don't offer wisdom from God's Word. They continue to tear them down and discourage them at their most vulnerable point, causing the suffering spectacles more pain and grief.

Sometimes spectacles cannot handle their trials or tests on top of all of the discouragement they are getting from other spectacles who should be comforting them. After all, they may start thinking, "They are running in the race too, and things like this are not happening to them." They may begin to believe what they are telling them. This can cause spectacles to lose all hope, to the point where they won't finish the race, or they will get out of the race and go back into the world. In extreme cases, they even wish they were dead.

This is why God was so angry with Job's three friends. In Chapter 42 verses 7–8, God tells Eliphaz, the first one who spoke, that he and his two friends did not speak the truth about Him as Job did. Here God, the referee, who watched the fight and listened to the heated arguments and debates, declares the winner. It was not Brother Eliphaz, or Brother Bildad, or Brother Zophar. Not even the young Brother Elihu, whom God does not even mention. Perhaps He held the other brethren responsible because they were older. But God said that Brother Job was right, declaring him the winner.

Now they have to go to the winner, Brother Job, and ask for forgiveness. The Lord told them to go to His servant Job and offer burnt offerings for themselves. God sent them to Job so he could pray for them, because He would not accept their prayers, only Job's. Job became their mediator because God was too angry with them to hear their prayers. In the same manner, God is angry with spectacles who harm, mistreat, give wrong advice, hurt, and cause other spectacles to suffer.

When Job prayed for his friends, his suffering was over

and he was given twice as much as he had before. According to verse 12, "...the LORD blessed the latter end of Job more than his beginning :..." God gave Job more after his calamities than he had before his calamities.

Notice how Job was forgiving and righteous and was willing and able to intercede in prayer for those who tormented him during his afflictions. Did you notice that God did not remove his suffering until he prayed for his friends? God wanted to see if Job would be upright before those who caused him grief during his trials. So Job hung up there, endured, passed his test, and lived a full life for many years.

While we are running on our racetracks and are confronted with hurdles to test our faith, when we cannot complete the jumps because they are *l-o-n-g* jumps, then we must wait with hope until our change comes so we can complete the jump. We must be ready to pray for and forgive the other spectacles who caused us grief, through their old nature, while we were enduring our trials. "...forgetting those things which are behind, and reaching forth unto those things which are before," (while we continue to) "...press toward the mark for the prize of the high calling of God in Christ Jesus." (Phil. 3:13–14).

God's Purposes for Trials or Tests

It has been stated many times in this book that throughout the New Testament, the apostle Paul compares the Christian race to an athletic competition. One reason is so we could better understand the trials of the Christian life. James 1:2–4 tells us we should count it all joy when we have various trials. Some trials were mentioned in this book just as examples, but throughout the Bible there are many, many more. Can you recognize any similar tests of trials or different ones you had experience with? Are you going through a test right now? What are some of the trials you have gone through or are going through? There are various kinds of trials; they can be in any form, come from anywhere, can appear in various ways, and can be numerous.

James tells us what our attitude should be while we are experiencing these various trials, which is that we should count all of them as joy. Why? Because the proving or testing of our faith gives us endurance or continuance capabilities. In other words, it is a spiritual workout. We explored the entire book of Job because it was an eye-opening example of what a spiritual workout looks like. It's similar to the athletes of various sports who work out regularly so they can have the endurance to compete. Verse 4 goes on to say that we should let the endurance have its complete workout in us. In other words, we should not fight the workout but let the workout do what it was designed to do.

Most athletes enjoy working out because they see the results; it has become a daily routine for them, like eating and sleeping. It is something they have to do to keep themselves fit. In the same way, when our faith is being tested we have to allow it to fulfill its purposes in us because it helps us to continue in the faith or develop endurance. When the workout is over, we will be complete because we have received what we needed.

Have you ever gone through a trial and felt spiritually stronger after it was over? That meant you allowed endurance to have its complete workout in you. That same endurance carried you through even another trial. When athletes first start working out, they may start off doing fifty push-ups and or sit-ups. Then they move on to a hundred; after a while they are able to feel that their workout was accomplished, because doing the hundred felt the same as fifty did. Now they can take it from a hundred to a hundred and fifty to two hundred with ease. If they never completed the fifty, they would not have had the endurance to make it to the hundred. The fifty sit-up or push-up workout compares to trials in that our trials are letting endurance have its complete workout. Then we can go on to the hundred sit-ups or push-ups. Just as workouts are beneficial to athletes, trials or tests are beneficial to spectacles in the Christians Olympics.

Persecution

The apostle Paul tells us in 2 Timothy 3:12 that "all that will live godly in Christ Jesus shall suffer persecution." The word for godly in the Greek *(eusebos)* means piously and reverentially. All Christians can live reverently in Christ and all who live reverently will suffer persecution. Persecution means to pursue, to go after, to capture, to chase, or to kill. That means that those who oppose Christ will pursue those who live reverently in Christ.

Just before Paul made that statement, he made mention of the persecutions and sufferings he came under and how God delivered him out of all of them, like the time Paul and Barnabas were cast out of Antioch where they were preaching. Then they went to Iconium to preach and later found out the people there were going to stone them, and they escaped. Then they went to Lystra where they preached. The people from Antioch and Iconium, the places where they were previously, came to Lystra, and this time they succeeded in stoning Paul. They dragged him out of the city thinking he was dead, but he was alive and rose up and went back into the city (Acts 13:14–14:20).

While we are on our racetracks living in a godly way in Christ, there will be those in hot pursuit of us. Jesus said in John 15 that if the world hates us, we must remember that they hated Him before they hated us. He added that as His servants, we are not greater than He was, so if they persecuted Him they will also persecute us (verses 18–21). We are partakers with Him in suffering, but there is a promise for those who do suffer: if we suffer with Him we shall reign with Him (2 Tim. 2:12). When Jesus becomes King, those who suffered with Him will reign with Him.

banishment

Banishment is another form of persecution. According to the book of Revelation, the apostle John experienced persecution while running on his racetrack, as most Christians did in the early church. He was sent to an island called Patmos "...for the word of God, and for the testimony of Jesus Christ." (Rev. 1:9). So there would be no misunderstandings, John quickly pointed out in this scripture the reason why he was on this barren island that was used for the banishment of criminals. It was not for some crime he committed—for speaking out against the government, protesting against social issues, or any of these kinds of things—but "for the word of God, and the testimony of Jesus Christ."

Sometimes as Christians, while we are running on our racetracks giving God's Word to the world and testifying about Jesus Christ, we may experience banishment. The word banish means to be put out of the country, to be exiled, sent away, dismissed, and ostracized, excluded from society.

Many Christians, especially in some foreign countries where other religions dominate the culture, are excluded from their families and countries because of their faith in Jesus Christ. In America, where Christianity is the dominant religion, banishment still occurs. It could come in the form of being friendless, being single, being without a church, or having our families disown us "for the word of God, and the testimony of Jesus Christ." We may not be put on an island as the apostle John was, but the ostracizers can make us feel as if we were. What I mean is that sometimes people can ignore us and act like they don't see us, as if we don't exist. This is how we can be exiled to an imaginary island, thus putting us on our own imaginary island of Patmos.

From what we see in the Scriptures, the apostle John

was alone with no church or believers to fellowship with, no family or friends. We can suffer physically while we are fighting in the race, if we get into a physical fight with someone causing an injury to our body for the cause of Christ. But much of our suffering is emotional, being alone and experiencing banishment. Sometimes emotional suffering can seem worse than physical suffering, or we can experience both physical and emotional suffering simultaneously. We may wish we had been yelled at, punched, or kicked, because the pain would have only last for a few minutes. But instead, we were ignored as if we were not there or banished, which is a deeper and longer hurt than a physical kick or punch.

purposes for the banishment

The apostle Paul, who was put in prison, and the apostle John stated publicly the reasons why they were persecuted. They knew the reason for their banishment. It is always important to know why we are suffering. It adds a purpose and offers a perspective on it, which helps us to endure it.

With banishment or any other type of suffering God always has a purpose for it. The obvious purpose is that when we are alone, God can certainly get our attention. We would be so surprised to see how much we are distracted by people and other things once we are forced through banishment to be alone with God. Truly that is what banishment is. We are separated from people but not from God. Things God wanted us to see and do we were not able to, because of the distractions of other people.

There are many things God wants us to do that we have to do alone. Sometimes banishment is the only way God can accomplish that. So don't feel forsaken if you look up one day and find that all of your family and friends have left you alone. Get to know Jesus more intimately and find out what He wants to teach you and what He wants you to do.

Whatever it is, it will benefit you and others.

While the apostle Paul was running on his racetrack, he was put into prison. During his first imprisonment, God gave him the words and time to write several letters to several churches. These letters became books in the New Testament of the Bible. They are the epistles to the Ephesians, Philippians, Colossians, and Philemon. His imprisonment helped to further the gospel. Other Christians saw his courage, and it helped them to gain the boldness to speak about their faith (Phil. 1:12–14).

Did you notice that Job also experienced a form of banishment? He was alone; all of his closest friends and family would have nothing to do with him. There is nothing like an illness to make everyone run away from you like the plague (smile). But God allowed it so Job could be alone with Him. When his trial was over, miraculously his closest family and friends greeted him and brought him gifts. They literally came out of the woodwork, as we would say. Where were they during his trials? It was as if there was a reason why they could not communicate with Job during his trials, as if they were being held back. This was part of the trial; God allowed Satan to keep his family and friends away from him.

Have you ever gone through banishment with no one to talk to but God, and as soon as that test was over, people suddenly appeared? For various reasons they were not available during your testing time. You felt abandoned and forsaken, but God allowed it to happen for a reason.

being reproached

Another form of persecution is **being reproached**. Being reproached for the name of Christ means to be accused of something or to be blamed for a fault or to be discredited for something we did not do or for something we have nothing to do with, just because we are Christians. For example, have you ever been accused of stealing something on your job and you never went near it or knew it was there? The persons or person who accused you knew you did not steal it, but because you were a Christian you were singled out and accused.

False accusations can be very severe, not only causing emotional suffering but psychological suffering as well. One of the hardest things we endure is being falsely accused, blamed, or discredited and made to look unrighteous when we are not. It can make us feel bad about ourselves even though it is not true. It can cause deep inner pain that leads to tears. Our old flesh will keep reminding us of all of the bad things that were said about us and none of the good.

Everyone wants to have a good reputation and not have their name destroyed. Satan, our competitor, will try to make us think we are not living a righteous life, because if we were no one would be able to falsely accuse us. This is how he tries to play tricks on our minds. He will have everyone believe we are guilty when we are innocent. He will have people say, "You must be guilty; everyone who is accusing you can't be wrong." Satan will continue to work on our psyche to try to get us to believe the lie that we must be guilty. If we allow him to continue he will even have us believing we are guilty.

Doesn't this sound familiar? How about Jesus Christ? Didn't they accuse Him of things He did not do, even though they knew He did not do them? Or maybe our neighbors make up stories about us that are just not true to discredit our righteous living for Christ. After the untrue story spreads throughout the neighborhood you can imagine your neighbors saying to one another, "I told you they were not so holy after all. They are supposed to be Christians." Didn't they make up—and aren't they still making up—stories about Jesus to discredit His deity?

Purposes for being Reproached

First Peter 4:14 says when this happens we should be happy because it means the "...Spirit of glory and of God..." rest upon us. That means others see the light of Christ shining through us. If they did not see Him in us, then we would have never been reproached and God would not have been glorified.

When people falsely accuse us and speak evil of us, we are told in 1 Peter 3:15–16 how to handle it: to "sanctify the Lord God in (our) hearts" and to always be ready to give an answer to every man. If we have a clear conscience, the evildoers who speak evil of us will be ashamed that they falsely accused our good behavior in Christ.

The meaning for the Greek word for conscience (*suneidesis*) is "(a) knowing with oneself." Having a good conscience means to know within ourselves we are suffering for well-doing for Christ's glory and not for evil. A good conscience is what should take charge over our emotions and our mind when we come under attack by our old flesh and Satan. That will help us to heal emotionally and psychologically through the suffering.

As a rule, if we are imitators of what is good or right, we will not be harmed or treated badly as Christians (1 Pet. 3:13). It is a guarantee though that if we do evil, we will suffer for it. On the other hand, if it is God's will for us to suffer, the Scriptures teach it is better to suffer for well-doing than for something we have done that was evil (1 Pet. 3:17). So when we suffer, the first thing we should ask ourselves is whether we are suffering for something we have done that was evil or for something we have done that was good. If it was for righteousness' sake (verse 14), we should be happy and not be afraid or troubled. We should not even think it strange but rejoice (1 Pet. 4:12–13), because we are partakers of Christ's suffering and have something in common with Christ.

Have you had things happen to you because you live a Christian life? It seemed strange, because you were imitating Christ. You were doing the right things; you should not have been treated that way. But now you can rejoice because you became a partaker in Christ's suffering for good. Now you can count it a privilege to go through sufferings as Christ did.

Some who are not Christians reading this chapter may be thinking, "Boy, Christians sure have it hard. They go through a lot." Some Christians may be thinking, "I'm not going through all of this" or "The moment it gets hard, I'll just get out of the race." What they don't understand is that whether they are Christians or not, or whether they are in the race or not, they will still have many problems and tribulations in this life; everyone suffers. But if we are Christians running in the race all of our difficulties are specifically designed, orchestrated, and allowed by God for our good and for our benefit (Rom. 8:28). So it is better to be on God's side and reap the benefits from our problems and sufferings since we are going to have them anyway.

First Peter 5:10 summarizes its exhortation on suffering for righteousness with the following conclusion: after we have suffered a while, it will perfect us, establish, strengthen, and settle us. If you have not experienced suffering yet as a Christian, you will one day. The magnificent result of suffering produces Christians who are well-adjusted and firm in their faith in Jesus Christ, resulting in a strong, established foundation.

CHAPTER 7

The Closing and Rewards Ceremonies

Closing Ceremony

The closing ceremony in the modern Olympic Games includes awards and salutations. The judges selected by the International Olympic Committee determine who will receive the awards. After each event the top three finishers receive their medals, the gold, silver, or bronze, at a medal ceremony. They stand on a platform while the flags of their countries are raised. The closing ceremony ends the competitions and includes fireworks and the extinguishing of the Olympic flames.

The rewards given to the winners of the Christian Olympics are similar to those given at the ancient games. For example the rewards for winning were wreaths or crowns made from leaves. According to a 2002 article from the Olympic Museum and Studies Centre in Lausanne, titled "The Olympic Games in Ancient Greece," the games were held at four different sites—Olympia, Delphi, Corinth, and Nemea—but not at all four in the same year.

Each city would have one winner who would receive the leaf crown for that city. At Olympia, the crown was made of wild olive leaves; at Delphi, laurel leaves; at Corinth pine leaves; and Nemea, wild cherry leaves.

Throughout the New Testament, the apostle Paul revealed to us that our rewards are also crowns. However, the crowns for the winners of the Christian Olympics are not made from anything perishable. They are crowns made of gold, according to Revelation 4:4. Just as the ancient games had different types of leaf crowns, the Bible speaks of five different types of gold crowns for the Christian Olympics. They are: 1) the Incorruptible Crown (1 Cor. 9:25); 2) the Crown of Rejoicing (1 Thess. 2:19); (3) the Crown of Righteousness (2 Tim. 4:8); (4) the Crown of Life (James 1:12, Rev.2:10); and (5) the Crown of Glory (1 Pet. 5:4).

While the modern Olympians receive their rewards after each event at a medal ceremony, the spectacles in the Christian Olympics will receive their rewards during the closing ceremony, when Jesus will give the crowns to the winners. No one knows when that will be, so Christians have to be faithful to God to the very end. We do know from the Scriptures that it will happen suddenly, without warning, in a moment, in the twinkling of an eye (1 Cor. 15:52).

Jesus Christ will descend from heaven to the sky with the sound of the trumpet. Christians who have died will be resurrected from the dead and, along with those who are alive, will be caught up together in the clouds to meet Jesus in the air (1 Thess. 4:16–17). We will see all of our families, friends, and others who have died, even those whom we have not seen for a long time. It will be the biggest reunion you'll ever want to see—Christians from all over the world, from every culture, joined together for the very first time in the middle of the air.

The return of Jesus will end the Christian Olympics. Just

as the fire is extinguished at the close of the modern Olympic games, the fire that symbolizes the Holy Spirit will leave this earth at the close of the Christian Olympics. The Holy Spirit dwells on the earth through Christians. When the Christian race or competitions are over and there will be no Christians on this earth, neither will there be the restraining power of Holy Spirit (2 Thess. 2:7). If it was not for the presence of Holy Spirit's restraining power or holding things down, the world would be worse off than it is now.

You can imagine the chaos that will occur around the world after the rapture, when the Christians are caught up to meet Jesus in the air. Remember there are Christians all over the world—from every nationality, every age, and every walk of life. After the rapture, when the Christians will be caught up to meet Jesus in the air, there will be a rewards ceremony in the sky.

The Rewards Ceremony

The rewards ceremony begins at the judgment seat of Christ: **"For we must all appear before the judgment seat of Christ, that each one may receive the things done in his body, according to what he has done, whether good or bad."** (2Cor.5:10, NKJV). In the modern Olympic games there are judges for each sporting event who decide which athletes will get the gold medals. They have been closely watching the athletes ever since they were selected to participate in the Olympics. Not only do they judge their athletic abilities but also whether they abided by the rules of the games.

It is the same with the Christian Olympics—only the judge is Jesus Christ, who has been closely watching every spectacle since they entered the competition. Because He is God, He has a greater advantage over other judges. He can actually see what we were thinking while we were running. He knows what was in our hearts while we are fighting, and

He knows what our motives were when we are wrestling.

As athletes have to appear before judges and stand before a platform individually to be judged, so it is for the spectacles in the Christian Olympics. We have to stand before God individually, and Christ will be sitting in the judgment seat, as a judge does in a courtroom. We will have to give an account of all of the good and all of the bad things we have done. We will have to answer to Him whether or not we did things to please Him or to please man, whether or not we were faithful to His Word and served Him with our spiritual gifts.

God will also judge our relationships. He will want to know if husbands loved their wives. Did wives submit themselves to their own husbands? Did children obey their parents? Did fathers provoke their children to wrath (Eph. 5:22–6:4)? Were we involved in immorality? How did we treat other people, especially those of the household of faith (Gal. 6:10)? Were we obedient employees to our employers? Did employers treat their employees fairly? This does not even scratch the surface of how God will examine our entire individual Christian life.

A record has been kept in heaven of every work we have done since we started running in the Christian Olympics.

God has laid the foundation of Jesus Christ, and what He expects of us is written in His Word. We have to follow it exactly. He determines if we have been faithful by using fire to sort out our works. We have either built on a foundation of gold, silver, and precious stones, or on a foundation of wood, hay, and stubble. After the fire, the spectacles whose works did not burn up will receive their reward. The spectacles whose works did burn up will suffer loss of rewards (1 Cor. 3:9–15).

The truth will be told. There will be no more secrets and no more pretending; everything will be brought to the light. Everyone will know who was faithful to God and who was not. Imagine the shame of suffering loss (1 John 2:28). To be reminded about not building on the foundation of Jesus Christ. It will be too late to change once standing before the judgment seat of Christ. To have lost the Christian race or competition and never again have the opportunity to "go for the gold crowns."

In sports there are championship games, tournaments, and finals where the winners win rewards. But they cannot be compared to the biggest sporting event of the world, the Olympic Games and winning the gold medals, or even the silver or bronze medals. It is the same in Christian service; there are times when God will reward us for being faithful to Him—with answered prayers or things we want or spiritual blessings—and there are times when people will reward us. But none of this is compared to the rewards of the gold crowns we will receive at the closing ceremony in the sky, at the closing of the most enormous and longest competition the world has ever seen—the Christian Olympics.

This is God's way of encouraging us to keep running in the Christian Olympics, being faithful in our service to Him until we reach the finish line. In the Olympic Games, only the finishers who finish first, or are the fastest or the strongest, who jump the highest or have the highest scores win the gold medals. But in the Christian Olympics all finishers will receive gold crowns. All we have to do is faithfully finish our race, just faithfully finish the course God has given to us, and we will be crowned with gold.

Athletes not only have to train, but they have to follow the rules in order to win the gold medals. It is the same in the Christian Olympics; we have to run according to the rules (2 Tim. 2:5) to get crowns just like the athletes do.

The Rules

First, we have to be faithful in our belief in the gospel of Jesus Christ, which we believed when we were saved. Some

Christians have allowed the devil to cause them to doubt, thinking that it was not their faith alone in the gospel that saved them, that there is something else they must add to it. This is the same way the devil tricked the Galatian church. They began to believe a person must be saved by keeping the law as well as by grace through faith. This is why the epistle to the Galatians was written, because they were departing from the true gospel. The apostle Paul said to them that they were running on their racetrack well. Then he asked them who hindered them from obeying the truth.

We have to be careful we do not allow anything or anyone to cause us to disbelieve in the Christian faith and God's Word. We also have to separate ourselves from those who preach another gospel or another faith and anything that is not true to God's Word. There are nationally renowned religious or so-called Christian speakers whom millions of people, even Christians, follow, but they preach another gospel. Some Christians are in churches and ministries where they know the truth of the Bible is not being taught, but they support them anyway.

Second, we have to confess our sins to God regularly so we can stay in fellowship with Him at all times (1 John 1:9). God cannot reward us if we have unconfessed sin in our lives. Another reason is so that we don't have to be chastised by God while we are running on the racetrack of the world (Heb. 12:3–15). The most embarrassing thing for children is to have their parents correct them or discipline them in public. We can remember how we felt when that happened to us; we felt like we wanted to climb into a hole or run away and hide. We were so embarrassed.

Well, it is the same way with our heavenly Father; when we are wrong, He will chastise us, and since we are spectacles, the whole world will see it. But we can avoid all of the embarrassment by just confessing our sins (1 Cor. 11:30–32). Do you know what this makes me think of?

Jonah. Remember when he tried to run away from God on a ship because he did not want to do what God told him to do? When God chastised him on the ship everybody knew about it. It's all recorded in Jonah.

Third, we must find out what our spiritual gifts are and utilize them. The church, the body of Christ, cannot function properly unless all of the gifts are in operation. These are the supernatural skills and abilities we use when we compete on the racetrack. Therefore, we must be certain we use the unique skills He gave us to the glory of God, and not try to use someone else's, in order to compete correctly.

And we must stay on our own unique racetrack that God has specifically designed only for us, by going where God sends us, not where we want to go or where others want us to go. We also need to be certain that we are qualified for any office we hold and that God has called us to that office, to His glory. This would put an end to all of the fighting, politicking, and scheming for positions and offices that goes on in our churches or ministries, just as it does in the world.

Many Christians will be so disappointed when they discover they did not qualify for a reward, mainly because of the three reasons we just discussed. They were following other people, doing things to be seen and praised by men for prestige, and trying to please everyone but God (Phil. 3:14).

The Rewards: What Are They?

The Five Gold Crowns

The spectacles whose works do not burn in the fire will win the Christian Olympics and will receive a reward. The rewards for finishing the Christian race or competition are five gold crowns. In the ancient Olympic Games only one person could win a crown at each of the four sites we mentioned earlier. In the Christian Olympics, every spectacle has an opportunity to win a crown. In the ancient games one athlete could win more than one or all of the four crowns. However, all spectacles in the Christian Olympics have an opportunity to win one, two, three, or four crowns, and some could win all five crowns.

The first crown is mentioned in 1 Corinthians 9:25–27, which is the Incorruptible Crown and is given to the spectacles who faithfully practice self-restraint while running on their racetracks in the Christian Olympics. Like the apostle Paul, they were able to develop the ability to be completely controlled by the Holy Spirit. They have control over their old nature, instead of the old nature having control over them. These are the Christians everyone makes fun of—even other Christians. They are called old-fashioned, boring, and too strict because they will not do anything that will hinder their run on their racetracks. Many times they are alone, misunderstood, and considered super-spiritual. If they think a movie, a television program, music, clothing, and other things will weaken their self-control or offend other spectacles, they will give it up for the sake of Christ.

The Crown of Rejoicing (1 Thess. 2:19–20) is the crown spectacles receive for leading souls to the saving knowledge of Jesus Christ while running on their racetracks and using their spiritual gifts. When the apostle Paul sees the Thessalonians at the coming of Jesus Christ, he will have joy knowing that because of his ministry they are in the presence of the Lord. When he receives his crown of rejoicing and he looks over and sees them, it will be just like receiving the gold crown. They are his crowns of rejoicing. It's like the feeling you get when you see someone you led to Christ. You can imagine the feeling you will get when you go to heaven and see souls that are there because of your witnessing.

The Crown of Righteousness (2 Tim. 4:8) is for all spectacles running on their racetracks as they fight, looking with great anticipation, love, and adoration for the return of

Jesus Christ. It is more than the feeling we get when we are suffering, going through persecution, or going through bereavement, times when we may want to die to be with Jesus or hope for the rapture to occur immediately. But for this crown, we have to love His appearing at any time, even when things are going well—even when we are young, have not yet done everything we wanted to do, have not finished something we have started, or have not visited all of the places we have ever wanted to visit. We must be willing to say in our hearts wherever we are and whatever we are doing in this life, "Even so, come, Lord Jesus" (Rev. 22:20), earnestly looking unto Jesus, who will be at the finish line.

The Crown of Life (James 1:12; Rev. 2:10) is for the spectacles who have the ability to endure trials even unto death. They are able to jump over the hurdles while fighting with wild beasts as they are running on their racetracks. When we go through trials especially to the point of death, it proves our love for the Savior. When you love someone, you will suffer for them even unto death, the same way Christ suffered for us; we then become partakers of His sufferings (2 Pet. 4:12–14). A perfect example is Stephen, who was fighting with wild beasts with his spiritual gifts and preaching to his enemies, who stoned him to death. He was the very first martyr and many have followed him. He fought a good fight and won because he kept the faith until death. It is believed that all of the apostles were martyred except for John.

The Crown of Glory (1 Pet. 5:2–4) is for the spectacles who are pastors that are utilizing this office in the church while running on their racetracks. Just being pastors does not automatically qualify to win the gold. How many members they have, how large of an edifice their place of worship is and the size of their choir or how well they sing has nothing to do with winning the Crown of Glory. First, spectacles have to have the spiritual gift of pastors-teachers (Eph.4:11) and meet the qualifications for that office (1

Tim. 3:1–7, Titus 1:5-16). Then they must be faithful shepherds who feed and look over God's flock—willingly, with a ready mind, and imitating the Chief Shepherd. According to 2 Timothy 4:1-5, they must be faithful preachers of God's Word in season and out of season. This is the only crown given for an office in the local church.

Ask Yourself These Questions

After discovering what the five gold crowns are, do you know if you have earned one? If so, which one or how many? Yes, it is possible to know right now if you have earned one or more crowns. The apostle Paul knew before he died that the Crown of Righteousness was waiting for him at the Judgment Seat of Christ. He knew in his heart how much he wanted Jesus to return (2 Tim. 4:8). He also knew he was going to get the Crown of Rejoicing because he knew of all of the souls that were saved because of his ministry (1 Thess. 2:19–20). The one crown he was not sure of was the Incorruptible Crown. He was successful at disciplining and training his body up to that point. But, since struggling with the old flesh is something done on a daily basis, he would not know whether he won that reward until his race was finally over (1 Cor. 9:25–27).

Should we be hoping and striving to get a gold crown like the athletes who go for the gold? YES! The apostle Paul tells us that in a race, all of the runners run even though they know only one is going to receive the prize. He is speaking of the ancient games where they only had one winner. How much more should we run, since in the Christian race or competition everyone has the opportunity to receive the prize? Then he goes on to say that we should have the same goals, and he gives us the authority for us to run and go for the gold crowns (1 Cor. 9:24). God knows we get tired and discouraged sometimes, so this is His way of encouraging us to run on to see what the end is going to be!

The Christian Olympics

If you carefully study the definition of each crown, you will see they were specifically designed by God to motivate and encourage us to run in the Christian race or competition. For example, if we strive for an "Incorruptible Crown" we will have a disciplined lifestyle, a consistent walk with God, a Spirit-filled life, and victory over the old self (old nature). Since Jesus has commissioned us to evangelize anyway (John 15:16), aiming for the "Crown of Rejoicing" only encourages us to do what we are supposed to do. We will witness to the unsaved more so we can have more joy when a soul is saved (Luke 15:7), and we will see the fruits of our labor throughout eternity. Souls are the only physical evidence of our labor that we will see in heaven.

If we are looking every day for Jesus to return, we will live a righteous life, so we will not be ashamed when He returns (1 John 2:28), which is the motivation for winning the "Crown of Righteousness." It is encouraging to know that all of the trials and tribulations we will endure, even unto death, are rewarded with the "Crown of Life." We will never suffer in vain. Striving for the "Crown of Glory" will remind pastors to examine their motives and remember that they are subordinate to the chief Shepherd and that the flock belongs to God, which will make them less concerned with the size of their membership or how well their choirs sing. But their concern will be directed towards being a faithful preacher of sound doctrine (Titus 2:1).

Is it possible to lose our crown? Yes. We cannot lose our salvation, but we can lose our crown. It is not like salvation; when we sin we can ask God to forgive us, according to 1 John 1:9. If we confess our sins, the blood continues to cleanse us from our sins, and we are forgiven. We can then continue to walk in fellowship with God. But with the rewards, once we see we have earned a crown and do something to lose it, we can confess our sins and be forgiven but still lose the crown. This is what 1 Corinthians 3:15 meant when it said that "he shall suffer loss; but he himself shall be saved." If we know that we have already earned one, we must take heed to the warning of Jesus who said, "Behold I come quickly: hold that fast which thou hast, that no man take thy crown" (Rev. 3:11).

Overcomers' Rewards

The 2002 article from the Olympic Museum and Studies Centre in Lausanne also points out that there were other symbols of victory besides the leaf crowns in the ancient games. The winners received red woolen ribbons and palm fronds to hold in their hands. The victorious athlete also became a hero and received benefits for the rest of his life.

When the Christian Olympics are over we will reign with Christ for a thousand years. Then there will be a new heaven and a new earth.

After the rewards ceremony in the sky, the spectacles will be in heaven with Christ for seven years. During that time, the world will be going through a seven-year tribulation period. At the end of this seven-year period, everyone in the world will see the spectacles who were in the Christian Olympics, now wearing their crowns. Just as the ancient Olympian winners were welcomed as heroes when they came back to their home towns, these spectacles, known as the bride of Christ, will come back to the earth with Christ to reign with Him for a thousand years. Jesus Christ will be the King sitting on His throne ruling the earth. Those spectacles who suffered with Him, were victorious, and were crowned will reign with Him.

During this time, special privileges and overcomers' rewards will be given to the spectacles that will last throughout eternity. This will be for those who were able to overcome particular obstacles and not yield to particular temptations during the Christian Olympics, just as the winners of the ancient games received various benefits for the rest of their lives.

We spoke in the previous chapter about how the apostle John experienced persecution in the form of banishment to the island of Patmos. But God had a purpose for him to be alone in exile. While he was there something miraculous happened; God revealed to him in a vision what had been hidden for centuries about heaven, the end times, and the future, and he was commanded by Jesus to write what he saw in a book. That book is called Revelation, the last book of the Bible.

The vision starts with him seeing Jesus, who tells him to write in a book what he sees and send it to the seven messengers of seven churches in Asia. Contained in these seven letters are recorded various overcomers' rewards and privileges for faithful service and obedience in addition to the five gold crowns. These letters were written to the churches to address specific problems they were having during that time. The book also foretold what the church would be like during our time.

God tells those who are running on their racetracks things He liked about their churches and the things He disliked. To those who were victorious or gained the victory over a particular sin were promised overcomers' rewards. If they chose not to obey, then God promised chastisement. This is the same thing God is telling the spectacles today as a church or as individuals, that if we overcome we will receive **overcomers' rewards** and privileges in the ages to come. If we disobey, chastisement will follow with no rewards.

The seven churches were in these seven cities of Asia: Ephesus, Smyrna, Pergamos, Thyatira, Sardis, Philadelphia, and Laodicea. One of the churches Jesus did not have to reprimand was the church in Smyrna. The letter to the messenger of this church was a very short one. This church was in poverty, going through tribulations, and under heavy persecution. In spite of all of this Jesus commends them, calling them rich. This was a letter of comfort for them because some of them were about to go through a great trial. Jesus tells them not to fear or become terrified of the things they are about to endure or suffer. The devil (who still has his same old job) will cast them in prison, and they will experience tribulation for ten days.

Their faith in Jesus Christ was going to be tested, and Jesus wanted them to be faithful to Him unto death. During this period many Christians willingly gave their lives for their faith in Christ. They were so rich spiritually that they walked in His footsteps and followed Him in suffering. These are the types of hurdles that spectacles jump over that are followed by death. But for other spectacles who jump over these hurdles, along with those in the church of Smyrna, Jesus promises to give them the **Crown of Life**.

And not only the Crown of Life; if they overcome or are victorious to the point of death then they "…shall not be hurt of the second death." (Rev. 2:11). The second death, according to Revelation 20:14, is the lake of fire, which is a lake that burns with fire and brimstone (Rev. 21:8). At the end of the thousand-year reign of Christ (known as the millennial reign), death and hell will be cast into the lake of fire. All unbelievers and Satan (the devil) will burn there forever.

When unbelievers die they go to hell, which is the first death. Then they are cast into the lake of fire, which is the second death. Therefore, unbelievers will die twice; when Christians die, they only die once, and the members of the church in Smyrna will only die once. When believers die they immediately go to heaven and have eternal life with Christ. The second death occurs after the thousand-year reign of Christ and His believers. So the members in the church in Smyrna who were faithful unto death will be reigning with Christ with their Crown of Life at the time of the second death.

Those who overcome will not be hurt by the second

death, which means something done wrong (inflicting of unmerited harm) or an injustice (unfair, unjust treatment of another, according to the Greek meaning) by the second death. The Bible does not explain what this means, but it is saying the second death could cause some type of wrong or injustice to spectacles who are going for the Crown of Life. It will keep them from getting this crown they deserve, because it will keep them from being faithful unto death. So there must be something about the second death (maybe it's the unsaved people who will experience the second death) that can hinder spectacles' trying to be faithful unto death to win this crown. Whatever it is, if they overcome or gain the victory by jumping over that hurdle to their death, then the second death is unable to cause them to lose their crown.

The next overcomers' reward is found in the message to Thyatira. Jesus promised the church in Thyatira that if they overcame and kept His works until the end that He will "...give power over the nations; and he shall rule them with a rod of iron; as the vessels of a potter shall they be broken to shivers: even as I received of my Father. And I will give him the morning star." (Rev. 2:26–28).

What was it that they had to overcome to the end? This church permitted a woman, who called herself a prophetess, to teach and seduce God's servants to commit sexual immorality and to eat things that were sacrificed to idols. But there were a few in the church who did not follow her doctrine. Jesus pronounced a punishment on her followers if they did not repent. Jesus offered encouragement for those who did not adhere to her doctrine to continue what they were doing.

This woman was compared to the Jezebel in the Old Testament, the wife of Ahab, king of Israel. Though Ahab was the king, his wife, who was very authoritarian, was running the kingdom instead of Ahab. She did not worship the true God; she persecuted His prophets, worshiped idols, and influenced others to do the same. Jezebel had four-hundred false prophets who ate at her table (1 Kings 16:31, 1 Kings 18—21; 2 Kings 9). Her authoritarian attitude was similar to that of the woman in this church; some of the people took her word as true instead of God's Word. When this happens, God is no longer the object of worship; the person whose words the congregation follows becomes their object of worship. God was angry with this church because they did not stop this woman from leading His servants astray.

This is the same thing God is warning the churches today. Churches may have people teaching and seducing their members to commit fornication, to worship them, other objects, and money instead of God.

God gave this woman time to repent of her immorality, but she did not. Now God gave those who were committing immorality with her time to repent or else they would be punished along with her. If they repented, along with those who were not involved, and they stayed faithful to God until they finished the race, they would be rewarded.

The reward will be given during the thousand-year reign of Jesus Christ. He will give them authority over the nations, just as He had received from His Father. In other words, the same authority His Father had given Him over the nations, He will give to them. Wouldn't it be something to have authority over the nations for a thousand years? But that's not all; there is another reward attached to this one. Jesus will give them the **"Morning Star."** Not only will they have power over the nations but also the Morning Star. What does it mean to be given the morning star, you may ask? First we have to look at who the Morning Star is. To find out we can look in Revelation 22:16, where Jesus says He is the "Bright and Morning Star." So the Morning Star is Jesus. Jesus is saying He will also give Himself to those in the church of Thyatira and other spectacles who overcame similar circumstances. They will have a closeness with Him that the other spectacles will not have. How wonderful it would be to have Jesus all to yourself.

In Revelation 3:5, we learn about another **Overcomers' Reward.** In the letter to the messenger of the church in Sardis Jesus says: **"He that overcometh, the same shall be clothed in white raiment; and I will not blot out his name out of the book of life, but I will confess his name before my Father, and before his angels."**

The church in Sardis was a church that had a name, a name other than the church in Sardis. Many churches are not just known for what they are called or the name that is placed on their building but also by what they want others to perceive them as, so they market themselves as such. The church in Sardis wanted to be known as the church that is alive. When people visited their church it had the appearance of a lively church, so they began to be known as the lively church. It is difficult to tell whether a church is alive by what we see or do not see when we visit.

This is just like visiting someone in their home; they will always show us the best side of themselves or what they want us to see. So if churches want people to think that they are alive they will create the appearance of a lively church. Especially now; there are so many new technologies out there that churches can create whatever atmosphere they want in the church.

We may not be able to tell if a church is alive, but there is someone who stands in the middle of every church who can. His name is Jesus Christ, and He could see right through the works of the church in Sardis. He told them they were dead. No matter how they gained the reputation as being an alive church, Jesus said they were dead.

What He was telling them was that their church and churches like them today do not show any signs of spiritual maturity. Jesus was able to find a tiny bit of spirituality there, but that it was almost dead. He tells them to wake up and strengthen or fix firmly the little they had left before that little bit died.

Just as Christians have to grow spiritually in their personal lives, the church has to grow spiritually as one body in Christ. If we don't grow, our spiritual life will become dead. When we have no fruit to show we are saved, we will act just like the world. Churches may have all the bells and whistles but still be dead in spiritual works. They are running in the race, but they are not doing any spiritual exercises.

Jesus tells them to remember what they have received and heard, to keep it and repent. If they don't wake up from their dead spiritual life, He will come upon them as a thief. If we are spiritually dead we will not be looking for God, so when He shows up He is not expected.

Jesus told them there are a few names in Sardis that have not defiled their garments, people who will walk with Jesus in white because they deserve it. There were a few members of that church whom God could see were spiritually mature. In churches today like this one, there would be a few people who could tell you the truth about their church, if you knew the right person to ask. They would say, "Our church is not all that people say we are....Let me tell you how things really are here."

For this church and other spectacles who overcome or gain the victory over this, during the thousand-year reign of Christ, they will be **Clothed in White Raiment** also. Even though they were acting like the unsaved with no spiritual fruit, **Jesus** will not blot their names out of the Book of Life, and He will confess their names before His Father and the angels. God will not disown them, because it is impossible for us to lose our salvation.

To the messengers of the church of the Laodiceans, Jesus says He knows their works; they are not cold and not hot, but lukewarm. He wished they were one or the other, but since they are lukewarm, He will spew them out of His mouth. The reason why Jesus calls them lukewarm is because this church said they were rich and wealthy, and they needed nothing, not even one thing. This church was so wealthy they did not have to pray and ask God or anyone else for anything. They had everything they needed, and if they wanted something they had accumulated enough money to buy it.

But Jesus asked them if they couldn't see that they were miserable and were like those who need kindness. He went on to tell them that they were not rich; they were poor, blind, and naked. Their wealth kept them from seeing their true condition. So Jesus showed them how spiritually poor and needy they really were. He told them to buy from Him gold tried in the fire so they could be spiritually rich; to buy from Him white raiment, which is righteousness, to cover the shame of their nakedness so they could be spiritually clothed; and to rub some eye salve in their eyes so they could spiritually see and understand.

Jesus wanted them to see that no matter how much money they had, they could not buy spiritual riches, spiritual clothing, and spiritual sight. This only comes from God, which He provides freely to those who seek Him. Because Jesus loves them, He rebukes and chastens them, telling them that now that they see how He sees them, they need to be zealous about it and repent. He will be standing at the door of the church of the Laodiceans knocking. If anyone hears His voice and opens the door, He will come in, and they will sup or have an evening meal together.

Like many of the churches today, Jesus has been put out of the church for various reasons. He is standing outside knocking, and if just one spectacle lets Him in, He will have fellowship and communion with him. One-on-one intimacy is what Jesus is looking for.

Did you notice that Jesus promised rewards to individual church members? Even if the church as a whole does not repent, each individual who does will be rewarded. So just because everyone in the church is disobeying God, we do not have to follow them; we need to follow God.

To this church and the spectacles who overcome and repent Jesus said He will **"...grant to sit with me in my throne, even as I also overcame, and am set down with my Father in his throne." (Rev. 3:21).**

During the thousand-year reign of Christ, the spectacles who overcome in this area will sit with Jesus in His throne, the same way Jesus overcame and sat with His Father in His throne. This is a prestigious position and the place where many spectacles wanted to sit. For example, the mother of Zebedee's sons asked Jesus if her two sons could sit with Him, one on His right hand and the other on His left hand in His kingdom (Matt. 20:20–24). What a privilege it would be after you overcame trials, tribulations, and persecutions to have this position of honor, to follow Jesus as an overcomer and sit down with Him in His throne.

The next group of Overcomers' Rewards will be for the spectacles after the thousand-year reign of Christ. When the Lord destroys the first heaven and the first earth with fire (2 Pet. 3:10–12) and creates the new heaven and the new earth, then the City of God, a Holy City, the New Jerusalem, which is suspended in the sky, will come down out of heaven (Revelation 21). In other words, you have to look up in the sky to see this city that God has "prepared as a bride adorned for her husband." This city has the glory of God as its light, and the city and the streets are made of pure gold.

The city has twelve gates with the names of the twelve tribes of the children of Israel written on them. The names of the twelve apostles of the Lamb are written in the twelve foundations of the wall of this city. This city has been prepared by God especially for those in the Christian Olympics, the spectacles, known as the bride, the Lamb's wife. This city will be the center of attraction, and everyone will be gazing at those who were in the Christian Olympics.

There are **Overcomers' Rewards** that will be received especially for the New Jerusalem. The first one we will mention is in the letter to the messenger of the church of Ephesus. Jesus knew their works, labor, and patience. They could bear those who are evil and have tried those who say they are apostles and are not. Even though they have not fainted, He has something against them; they have left their first love.

Jesus gives them a warning—if they do not remember where they fell, they must repent and do the first works; He will come quickly and remove their candlestick or church. But they hated the deeds of the Nicolaitans, which He also hated. They were those who profess to be Christians, but they lived immorally. The reward given to those who overcome is the opportunity **"to eat of the tree of life."**

Remember the Tree of Life that was in the Garden of Eden and was mentioned in Genesis? Eve and Adam did not choose to eat of the "Tree of Life"; they yielded to Satan's temptation and ate of the "Tree of Knowledge of Good and Evil" (this is when Satan started his first temptation of mankind), which was the only tree that God forbade them to eat from. When they disobeyed God they were driven out of Eden, and God placed a cherubim and a flaming sword at the entrance to Eden to keep everyone away from the Tree of Life (Genesis 3).

But the overcomers of the church of Ephesus will have the special privilege of eating the fruit of the Tree of Life. He says to spectacles today who no longer have Him as their first love that if they make Him their first love again, they will be given this special reward. In the New Jerusalem you will have the privilege of eating from the tree of life, which is in the middle of God's paradise. Not only is there a new heaven, a new earth, and a New Jerusalem, but there is a new paradise. According to Revelation 22:2, the Tree of

Life yields twelve types of fruit every month, and the leaves are for the healing of the nations. God has preserved this tree just for you.

The next group of **Overcomers' Rewards** awarded after the thousand-year reign of Christ is mentioned in the letter to the church in Pergamum. Jesus says in the letter to the messengers in this church that He knows their works, where they dwell, and even where Satan's seat is. He knows how they hold fast to His name and have not denied His faith. Even during the days when Antipas was slain among them, they were still faithful. But Jesus said He still has a few things against them, because some of them hold the doctrine of Balaam, the union of the world and the church. Some also hold the doctrine of the Nicolaitans, which He hates. He tells them to repent or He will come quickly and fight against them with the sword of His mouth. But to him who overcomes, He will give "...to eat of the hidden manna, and will give him a white stone, and in the stone a new name written, which no man knoweth saving he that receiveth it." (Rev. 2:17).

Do you remember the manna that was mentioned in Exodus? When the children of Israel came out of Egypt and journeyed through the wilderness, they began to complain about not having food like they had in Egypt. So the Lord heard their complaints and caused quails, which are birds, to cover their camp every evening for them to eat. These are the types of birds that nest on the ground. Also, every morning the Lord sent them bread from heaven to eat, which they called manna. It was a miracle the way the bread came down like rain every morning, just enough for each person for that day. This was the way God provided bread for the children of Israel for the forty years they were in the wilderness. Psalm 78:24–25 refers to the manna as "corn of heaven" and "angels' food."

Manna was white and tasted like wafers or cakes made

with honey. Imagine eating bread that God made fresh for you every morning. The Lord commanded the children of Israel to keep a portion of the manna in a golden pot, to show future generations how the Lord fed them in the wilderness (Exod. 16:1–36). This golden pot of manna was set aside and was put in the Ark of the Covenant (or testimony), which was located in the Tabernacle, in the Holy of Holies behind the second veil.

Only the priest was allowed to enter the Holy of Holies and only once a year, with a blood sacrifice for himself and the people (Heb. 9:1–7). Since the Holy of Holies is now in heaven, so is the manna hidden there. For the overcomers of the church in Pergamum and other spectacles, they will have the privilege of eating the hidden manna. That's not all; the overcomers will be given a white stone that will have a new name written in it that only they will know.

God's rewards to you are very personal and special. How special you will feel to have a new name that no one knows but you and God! Even sweethearts who have given each other nicknames they use privately share them with someone else eventually. But there will be no one who can call you by your new name in the new heaven and earth, because no one will know it but you and Jesus. Can you wait to go to heaven to hear God call you by your new name?

To the church of Philadelphia Jesus says He knows their works and sets before them an open door that no man can shut. Once shut, no man can open it. Because they have a little strength and have kept His word and have not denied His name, He will make them of the synagogue of Satan to worship before their feet and to know He has loved them. Because they have kept the Word of His patience, He will keep them from the hour of temptation. He is coming quickly, and they must hold fast to what they have so no man takes their crown. This indicates that up to this point they have earned a crown and they can also receive other rewards.

There is nothing about this church that Jesus condemns. He just wants them to continue to do what they are doing until He comes. If they continue and go through the door He has opened for them, they will be given Overcomers' Rewards. Jesus says to the overcomers of this church: "…I will make a pillar in the temple of my God, and he shall go no more out: and I will write upon him the name of my God, and the name of the city of my God, which is new Jerusalem, which cometh down out of heaven from my God: and I will write upon him my new name." (Rev. 3:12).

The winners of the Olympic Games in ancient Greece became heroes in their home towns. Sometimes the citizens made coins with the winners' images on them in order for them not to be forgotten and to make them known all through the Greek world. The winners had the privilege of having statues made of themselves. They could ask poets to write about their unusual skills (Olympic Museum and Studies Centre, Lausanne, 2002).

The overcomers of the church in Philadelphia and other spectacles in the Christian Olympics will be made a pillar in the Temple of God. A pillar is a column. Have you seen buildings that have columns that support the building? They are part of the building, holding it up. When the Scriptures speak of pillars, though, they are referring to a single pillar like a monument. You will be a living monument. Just as a pillar or column is a permanent supporting fixture in a building, you as a monument will be permanently on display. This is what Revelation 3:12 means when Jesus says "he will go no more out." Everyone in the new heaven and earth will be going in and out to see God and Jesus, who are the Temple (Rev. 21:22). But you will not have to go out, because only you have been given the privilege of having a permanent position, to be a monument right beside God and Jesus. The name of God will be written on you, the monument, by Jesus.

Also the name of the city of God, the New Jerusalem, will be written on you. The New Jerusalem comes from God out of heaven, and it never touches the earth. As we mentioned before it is suspended in the sky between heaven and earth. That is why the angel had to take the apostle John to a "great and high mountain" in order to see this city (Rev. 21:9–27). This is where you will be a permanent monument that everyone will be looking at with the name of God and His city written on you. Since the temple is God and Jesus, and you will be a monument (pillar) in the Temple of God, when everyone sees God and Jesus, they will see you right beside them.

But that's not all; Jesus will also write on you His new name. Jesus has many names that are found in the books of the Bible, from Genesis to Revelation. For example, in Revelation some of His names are the Alpha and Omega, the Almighty, Faithful and True, the Word of God, the Lamb, the Root and the Offspring of David, the Bright and Morning Star, and the King of Kings and Lord of Lords. In the New Jerusalem, He will have a new name that will only be written on you.

Did you notice that all of the rewards are personal rewards? Over and over again Jesus repeated the phrases "to him that overcometh" or "he that overcometh" before He revealed what the rewards were. His message was for the whole church, but the rewards were for each individual who gains the victory. They were not to wait to see if everyone else in the church was going to follow Jesus' commands, but their decisions were between them and Jesus individually. The church as a whole may or may not overcome and get the rewards, but individuals can. No matter what everyone else in the church may or may not be doing, that cannot prevent the individual from being rewarded.

When Jesus went back to heaven, He promised He would prepare a place for us (John 14). In this life, we make decisions affecting where and how we will spend eternity.

We make decisions about whether to spend eternity in heaven or in hell. Since we are eternal beings, we will all live forever in the place we have chosen. We who have made the decision to spend eternity in heaven can also choose how we will live there and what positions we will have when we get there. (Those who have chosen hell can determine in this life how much they want to suffer in hell forever...but that's another subject).

This life, which is just a preparation, is very short compared to eternity, and everything we do in this life determines how we will live in heaven. Once we get to heaven, eternity begins. Preparation time will be over, and it will be too late to make any changes. We can decide right now whether we want to be pillars in God's temple or be satisfied just to be the ones who are looking at those Christians who have permanent positions as monuments right beside Jesus and God, having the name of God, His city, and Jesus' new name written on them—to be called by a new name that no man knows, to have the privilege to eat of the hidden manna that is still moist and the twelve manner of fruits from the Tree of Life, or to just drool as you watch the other Christians lick their lips and suck their teeth. You decide.

You can be among those who sit with Christ in His throne, reign with Him, and wear white garments. It's all up to you; it's never too late to get back in the race if you have gotten out of it. God rewards those who diligently seek Him. He will reward you for following His commands. Whatever it may be that is keeping you from overcoming won't be worth it when you get to heaven. Is it worth going through all of the difficulties of this life to then get to heaven and not be able to experience all of the privileges there? After all, we will be in heaven for an eternity, and what we traded in for heavenly rewards is only going to perish.

EPILOGUE

The Competition That Made the Judge Stand Up

At this time, Jesus does not have His own throne; He is still sitting on the right hand of God watching us run up, down, and around on our individual racetracks, waiting for the day to reward us. But there was one time recorded in the Scriptures when He was watching a particular racetrack. He saw a spectacle fighting with the wild beast. He was sitting in His usual seat on the right hand of His Father, but He had to **get out of His seat and stand up!**

Once in a while at a sporting event an athlete does something so spectacular that the judges are so amazed that they have to get out of their seats and stand up. This is what happened: just before Stephen was stoned to death, as he finished preaching God's Word, he looked into heaven and saw the glory of God and Jesus standing on the right hand of God. When he told the council that he saw the heavens open and Jesus, whom they rejected, standing on the right hand of God, they were so convicted they covered their ears and stoned him to death. If you read the entire seventh chapter of Acts, you can see why Jesus stood up. Stephen was able to use his two-edged sword to pierce the hearts of the enemies of the cross of Christ, winning the fight with the wild beast.

Are we running so well on our racetracks that Jesus has to get out of His seat and stand up?

The most enormous and longest competition the world has ever seen, the Christian Olympics, one day will suddenly come to its end at the closing ceremony in the sky.

Pray This Prayer

IF You Want To Become A Member Of The Christian Olympics Pray This Prayer!
Dear God:
I believe that I am a sinner. I am sorry. Please forgive me for my sins. I do not want to go to hell when I die, but have eternal life in heaven with you. I believe in my heart that Jesus Christ is God, who became a man to die in my place. I receive His death and the blood that He shed to wash my sins away as payment for the penalty of my sins. I believe in my heart that you raised Jesus Christ bodily from the grave. I now receive your gift of eternal life. Thank you for saving me from hell because of Jesus. In His name I pray. Amen.

If you prayed this prayer from your heart and you were sincere, then you now have eternal life. You have been Saved from hell.
"That if thou shalt confess with thy mouth the Lord Jesus, and shalt believe in thine heart that God hath raised him from the dead, thou shalt be saved." Romans 10:9.

Now that you are saved, you have become a Christian, you have been born again (John 3:3-7). You are in the Christian Olympics. The Holy Spirit now lives inside of you and will never leave you (Ephesians 1:13, Hebrews 13:5, John 14:16). God wants you to join a church that believes in the teachings of this prayer. And will baptize your entire body in the name of the Father, The Son, and the Holy Ghost (Matthew 3:13-17, 28:19). Also, to partake of Holy Communion, the bread and the fruit of the vine, to remember Jesus' death (1Corinthians 11:23-34, Matthew 26:26-29). Pray, talk to God daily, read the Holy Bible, and God will speak to you daily. When you sin confess it to God (1 John 1:9). Keep the faith and you will receive crowns of gold at the Reward Ceremony in the sky.

About the Author

A marathon runner in the Christian Olympics for many decades, S. E. Gregg is the founder of Sound Doctrine Christian Ministries. As a gifted Bible teacher, writer, and award winner, Gregg has authored and published the bestselling books *Evangelism Counseling: How to Counsel People About Salvation* and *The Christian Olympics-Going for the Gold Crowns.* The salvation tract "God Became a Man" was designed my S. E. Gregg and over 100,000 have been printed in the Burmese language.

> If you would like information on purchasing the above titles, have an author interview request or for speaking engagements go to:
> SoundDoctrineMinistries.org
> E-mail Address:
> Resources@SoundDoctrineMinistries.org
> Or write: Sound Doctrine Christian Ministries
> P. O. Box 407, Wynnewood, PA 19096
> Or go to: ChristianOlympics.org
> E-mail Address: Victory@ChristianOlympics.org

www.ingramcontent.com/pod-product-compliance
Lightning Source LLC
Chambersburg PA
CBHW050553300426
44112CB00013B/1892